HOW
TO
KEEP YOUR
MAN
MONOGAMOUS

HOW TO KEEP YOUR MAN MONOGAMOUS

Alexandra Penney

BANTAM BOOKS
NEW YORK • TORONTO • LONDON • SYDNEY • AUCKLAND

HOW TO KEEP YOUR MAN MONOGAMOUS
A BANTAM BOOK 0 553 40169 6

First publication in Great Britain

PRINTING HISTORY
Bantam Books edition published 1990

Copyright © Alexandra Penney 1989

Corgi Books are published by Transworld Publishers
Ltd., 61–63 Uxbridge Road, Ealing, London W5 5SA, in
Australia by Transworld Publishers (Australia) Pty. Ltd.,
15–23 Helles Avenue, Moorebank, NSW 2170, and in New
Zealand by Transworld Publishers (N.Z.) Ltd., Cnr. Moselle
and Waipareira Avenues, Henderson, Auckland.

Printed and bound in Great Britain by
Cox & Wyman Ltd., Reading, Berks.

For John Brulport Penney
and
For Dr. John B. Train

The women who are deserted
are the women who love.
The women who keep their lovers
are those who practice the arts of love.

—BALZAC

ACKNOWLEDGMENTS

I owe the truly brilliant team at Bantam many, many thanks: Linda Grey, Steve Rubin, Stuart Applebaum, plus Jack Hoeft, Matthew Shear, Nina Hoffman, Jill Bennett, Don Weisberg, everyone in the managing editor's office, and of course, at the top, the ultissimo Alberto Vitale.

Deborah Futter, whiz-editor and special pal, deserves a huge thank-you.

Three friends deserve official acknowledgment: Maggie Scarf for pulling me through, Margaret Staats Simmons who saw the problems and helped mend them, and Susan Dooley who provided optimism, good faith, good cooking, and great editorial counsel.

Other friends gave generously of their time and support: Beth Brown, Myrna Blyth, Erin Dracos, Harriet Fier for her astute advice, George Friedman who offered many "cutting edge" comments, Ellen Howard, Robert Lang, my patient and indefatigable researcher, Michael Martell and Alice Fried Martell, my good doctor Allen Mead, Gloria Nagy for her jokes, cartoons, and phone messages, Carolyn Seely, Deborah Sharpe, Nicholas von Hoffman for his morning pep talks and devotion to the monogamic ideal. And, as always, a huge thank-you to the ever-delightful Tuna B. Fish who, I'm sure, will land the elusive Ambrose T. Gumbs.

I'm very grateful to the New York Society Library which provided peace, calm, a special typing room, and a helpful staff.

Susan and Harrison Young, superlative host and hostess at "Casa Giovane" where I revitalized and rewrote, deserve my warmest thanks and appreciation.

Great quantities of gratitude go to the incomparable Lynn Nesbit—this book would not have existed without her. She was with me every word of the way.

CONTENTS

1   Introduction   1

2   The Sex Equation   10

3   "Monogamy? Is That a Kind of Wood?"
    He Asked   16

4   Men Who Stay, Men Who Stray   21

5   Hotel Room, Chicago   40

6   The Long-Term Lover, the One-Night Stander,
    and the Occasional Strayer   56

7   When, Where, and How He's Most Likely
    to Be Unfaithful   68

8   The Other Woman: What Does He See
    in Her?   76

9   The Boy, the Adolescent, the Man   87

10 Our Secret Selves   94

11 Hungry Hearts   100

12 How to Get Your Man to Be Monogamous   113

13 Love Passages   125

14 The Peril Points   131

15 How to Satisfy a Man Sexually 143

16 Five Sex Mistakes Most Women Make
(and the Sixth Deadly Sexual Sin) 154

17 "I'll Never Forgive You!" 165

18 Diamonds and Orange Juice 176

ONE

Introduction

"In my wildest, most romantic dreams I couldn't have had a better beginning to a relationship. He'd seen me at a restaurant where a group of us hung out after work and asked a mutual friend for my name. Two days later he called and we made a date for the following Saturday. It was 1974 and the height of the oil crisis. We waited in line for gas at an Exxon station for two hours, talking and drinking wine that he was bringing to a party—but we never made it there. Sex was fantastic. It was a whirlwind courtship. We fell madly in love.

"He was attractive in the extreme. Curly-haired, blue-eyed, tall, handsome as sin. But he was more than good-looking. Smart, aesthetic, very independent, and he genuinely liked women. He had this incredible male quality about him.

"Women were always coming on to him and calling him. I was shocked at how aggressive they were. But he would always be friendly and neutral, neither en-couraging nor discouraging. The calls made me crazy, but I knew he loved me. He was as attentive and ro-mantic and smitten as you could ever want a man to be.

"We worked lunatic hours. Sometimes I'd get to his place at two in the morning and he'd be sleeping. Sometimes I'd be there by ten at night and he'd come in much later. It was a wonderful time for us. We'd give big parties—he had an old, rambling house; I loved to cook, we both loved to have fun.

"He often invited his entire office to these parties. One of the women who worked with him was from Berkeley and she always showed up. She was not particularly attractive. She had long hair, a young child, an odd name—Lucrezia. And she wore that perfume Shalimar. She was brittle, a little harsh, but smart, no doubt about that.

"This woman would call him and he was always teasing about her name. At our parties it was clear—to me at least—that he felt uncomfortable around her. He'd say 'Why doesn't she leave me alone?' but I took her aggressiveness in stride.

"I was working late one night and called him at his office and at the house a couple of times, but I didn't reach him. We'd talked earlier in the day, and I knew he was going down to his company's headquarters in Berkeley. It was past midnight and I headed over to his place, as I always did on a very late night, and I just collapsed on his bed from sheer exhaustion. When he went to Berkeley, he'd usually sit around having a drink and guacamole with some pals from the office while he waited for the traffic to clear, so I figured he'd be home in about a half hour or so.

"But he didn't show up.

"Then I started to worry. He'd fallen asleep on the road, there had been an accident. But in my gut I knew it wasn't true. He was a good driver, competent, careful.

"I didn't sleep at all. At about nine-thirty in the morning, I called his friend Steve in Berkeley, casually saying I was looking for him. I didn't want to sound in any way like a jealous, hysterical woman. I didn't want to be uncool, it was the worst sin.

" 'Well,' he said innocently, 'Paul and Lucrezia and I went out for a drink and I had to leave early—' And then I *knew*.

"I was sitting on the edge of his bed. I got up and my knees were shaking. I couldn't stand and I couldn't breathe. I had real trouble breathing.

"I cleaned up the bed as if I'd never been there, washed out the teacup I'd used the night before, put it away and then went home.

"I was a complete and total mess, but I had to go to work. . . . I wasn't angry. I was devastated and betrayed.

"He didn't phone me. Finally, about ten, I called him and he got on the phone and nonchalantly said, 'Hi.'

"I said I just wondered how you were and if you'd had a late night, and he said yes, he'd had a late night. There was an incredible awkward silence and I said nothing. I could tell he was uncomfortable, and then I said I had to be at a meeting and we hung up. I was shaking and couldn't breathe when I got off the phone.

"I had thought a lot about Lucrezia and I felt he had been with her. It wasn't paranoia. Here was a woman with a very young child and a full-time job, and she was adjusting a tight schedule to sit around sipping drinks with her colleagues. It didn't add up. There was no professional need for her to do this. And then there was also the fact that she was always calling Paul about some irrelevant matter.

"Somehow I muddled through the morning. I was so strung out, a friend gave me a Valium. I'd never had one before and I'm very sensitive to drugs. It made me sleepy so I went home, but I have no recollection of driving—I stayed in bed all afternoon.

"That evening he called and he said, 'I've been trying to reach you at the office. Where have you been?' I said

I'd been sleeping, and he told me he wanted to come to my apartment for dinner.

"I was incredibly upset but determined to be cool, to be an understanding mature woman. Of course the minute he walked through the door, I burst into tears.

"I told him I knew who he was with and he said 'I'm a grown man. I had a few drinks. It's no big deal. She doesn't mean anything to me. I love you.'

"We had a long talk and I remember thinking it was all a big excuse. We stayed together for several years after that, but the part of me that was unsuspicious and trusting was gone. . . . I'm sitting here telling you this, it all happened over a decade and a half ago, and right now as I think about it, my knees feel weak, it's hard to breathe."

Janice Fromm is the woman who told me the story you just read. Her words are excerpted from a two-hour interview we had in San Francisco in the spring of 1986. Janice was not recounting a rare experience: Millions of women have had their husband or lover or boyfriend involved with another woman, and every one of us feels the same anguish, the same raw, sickening dread and searing pain that Janice vividly described when we sat in her calm, Wedgwood blue living room more than ten years after it had all happened.

Today the issue of monogamy is a headline-maker and career-breaker, but to women, fidelity has always been the nerve center of a relationship. In an AIDS-dominated environment, monogamy becomes an even more explosive issue. Ghastly though the facts of the disease are, widespread infidelity is surviving the AIDS crisis intact.

It's generally agreed that, today, around 50 to 65 percent of men are unfaithful. (Some researchers have raised the figures to 70 percent or more.) To put it plainly: *The odds are high that he will cheat on you.*

Why is this so?

It seemed clear to me that men themselves could best answer that crucial question but no one, to my knowledge, had asked men what monogamy was all about for them. So I decided to interview at least two hundred males in order to discover exactly what it is that makes a man stray—and, much more importantly, what would make him stay.

It wasn't my intention to become a social scientist, nor am I a scholar or statistician: I'm a reporter and researcher and a woman who is personally and professionally interested in monogamy. The questions that I asked the men I interviewed are those that I and other women want answered.

I started out by asking both my male and female friends and colleagues to give me the names of men whom they thought would be willing to talk about monogamy. My only provisos: I should not know the person or come into contact with him socially or professionally after the interview.

I received a raft of responses and I plunged in and started calling people and making appointments. After the first dozen interviews in New York, I flew out to Los Angeles, San Diego, and San Francisco. The men that I talked with in California gave me other names, and I started branching out to cities and towns across the country.

I conducted just under two hundred formal, in-depth interviews on monogamy, each of which lasted from an hour to three or more hours. In addition to these, I spoke to other men more briefly, getting "quick takes" on the subject.

Though this is not a scientific sampling, it does include men from a wide variety of ethnic, economic, religious, and educational backgrounds. The ages of the men ranged from nineteen to seventy-seven.

In addition to men, I interviewed psychiatrists, clinical psychologists, sociologists, marital and pastoral counselors, divorce lawyers, and of course, other women. I've also plumbed the latest surveys, statistics, analyses, and most current articles on gender research, monogamy, and infidelity.

In the two and a half years that it took to dissect monogamy, I was aware of what I came to think of as the *honesty quotient*. It's well known that most large surveys tend to be self-selective; for example, people who send in magazine questionnaires do so because they *want* to answer those questions, because they may be more interested—or have had more experience—with the subject than those who simply toss the survey into the trash can. Men and women who have problems with fidelity may be more likely to volunteer to cooperate than those who are happily monogamous. And, of course, this skews the numbers in various ways. In addition, it's also common for people to distort, exaggerate, or just plain lie to researchers about the hypersensitive subject of infidelity/monogamy.

I can't say with absolute certainty that the men I interviewed in depth told me the truth. I was a stranger asking extremely personal questions. The nature of the subject is furtive, covert, and it is difficult for even the most cavalier man to discuss the ways in which he has betrayed his mate.

As I worked my way back and forth across the country, I tried to conduct each interview in circumstances where the man could relax. For some, this was an office setting. For others, an anonymous environment, a restaurant, a bar, a coffee shop, was more comfortable. In a dozen cases I had to settle for interviews by phone.

For my last three books I've interviewed men on romance, love, and sex. Monogamy was an even tougher subject than sex for most men to talk about because of the complicated and often painful feelings it evokes. But slowly, by gaining trust, sensitively asking the most probing questions—and promising that each man's identity would remain unrevealed—I believe intimate truths were told. The names of everyone I've interviewed are changed, but their words are unaltered.

Monogamy is one of the most emotionally charged problems in a love relationship, but it is also an issue with many complex facets—cultural, philosophical, religious, and moral—and although I was intrigued by the fascinating polemics that surround the subject in its broadest scope, I stuck to my basic objective: *What does it take for a man to be monogamous?*

As the interviews began to accumulate, so did certain patterns and mechanisms. Men are not born to stray—or stay. Neither are women. Something happens to make us monogamous. The men I talked with, plus the interviews with experts and the research that I did, gave me valuable new information on what that "something" is. This information is what every woman needs in order to comprehend today's man and enjoy a monogamous relationship—and YES, I found that an exciting fulfilling one-on-only-one relationship is very much possible to have with your man.

What I discovered about monogamy is what the rest of this book is about. But before you read on, it's very important to underscore that a man doesn't fool around because of something *you've* done—or not done. It has nothing to do with whether you're sexy enough or worthy enough or smart enough. You will learn that a man strays because certain of his primary needs are not being met—emotional and sexual needs that you probably are not aware of (and which I'll target and analyze in detail later). As a sophisticated, contemporary woman, you can satisfy those needs without sacrificing your own hard-won self-esteem and self-respect. Most importantly, in fulfilling his needs, you will be securing the most primal emotional and sexual needs *you* have: love, intimacy—and monogamy.

I'll begin by explaining why monogamy is so crucial to women, and then we'll go on, in the first part of the book, to listen to the surprising, fascinating, and often shocking things that men have to say about monogamy. You'll see why most men think and feel *very differently* about it than we do; you'll realize how many men have a sliding definition of monogamy and why they have to maintain this doublethink; we'll probe the issue of monogamy and a man's age and life-style; the conditions in which he's most likely to stray; what he says about the "other woman" and precisely what attracts him to her; and you'll learn exactly when in a relationship the "natural monogamy period" ends—and why. We'll explore the world of the genuinely committed monogamous man and counterpoint that with the disturbing profiles of "womanizers" and how to spot them; you'll find out about hidden one-night stands, as well as the men who believe in "dual monogamy," and the "occasional strayer"—experts agree that he's the kind of man you're most likely to be married to or living with.

After we've heard from men, we'll delve into fascinating new psychosexual territory: the ego structure of today's man and what his needs are and the ego structure of today's woman and what her needs are. The anatomy of male and female egos is not the same. Men have certain ego needs and women have others—but after you grasp the forces on which each is constructed, you'll realize that it's possible to reconcile these differences.

What does all this have to do with monogamy? As you will see, everything.

Once you become aware of male and female ego structures, you'll be able to understand a surprisingly simple principle—that of fulfilling psychosexual needs—both his and yours. Most importantly, this principle can be translated into a practical, wonderfully effective strategy that you can use immediately to make your own relationship monogamous.

The premise of this book—satisfying ego needs—may be disturbing to modern women who don't subscribe to the idea of strategizing and modern men who don't like to believe that it's still necessary. But despite the good and sincere intentions of today's men, the fact is that it is usually the woman who ultimately takes responsibility for, and nurtures, intimate relationships. Contemporary research as well as my own findings substantiate this. Most of the men I've talked with have expressed a genuine willingness to meet women halfway, but they're also aware that, in reality, intimate relationships can be a different matter. "I'd like to believe I'll be an equal partner in making a marriage work," said one twenty-seven-year-old man. "I'm going to be trying in my own ways. But I see that in real life, the woman still bears more of the burden."

All through this book you'll be reading case histories based on my interviews and research—these illustrate how using this simple strategy of satisfying ego needs can work in your everyday world. You'll also find suggestions, solutions, tips, and specific sexual material that tells you exactly what your man responds to. All of these interviews and all of this information has one purpose: to help you create and maintain an intimate relationship that's rich, romantic, adventurous, fulfilling—and monogamous.

TWO

The Sex Equation

"What," flashed Oprah Winfrey, "do women *really* want?"

"Men," I shot back, and she grinned.

If I hadn't been on a television show, I would have sat back and pondered all sorts of aspects and issues that relate to that primal Freudian query before spilling out an answer. On the two-hour flight back home, I did some hard thinking, and I landed with the same conclusion: Yes, I believe what women really want is men. We want a great many other things in addition—children, career, a spiritual and intellectual life—but I believe that a majority of women would agree, probably not publicly though, that a man is first on the list.

Obviously, we want and need men to propagate the human race. But there was more to my answer than that. There is a requisite that women possess that I believe is beyond biological and beyond Oedipal—and only men can fulfill it: Most of us want, need, and depend on love and emotional and physical intimacy from men.

A significant amount of recent research confirms this idea. New psychological studies are focusing on the area

of intimacy as it pertains to women and their relationships with men. Surveys substantiate that the closest
kind of association, the deepest kind of loving contact,
the revelation of our true nature and the reception of
another's—in a word, intimacy—is crucially important for
a woman's psychological well-being.

For a woman, monogamy is integrally entwined with
that kind of connectedness and intimacy. The men with
whom we allow ourselves to be truly intimate have our
complete trust and love. We believe that we have entered into a physical and emotional bond with them that
is inviolable. That bond of monogamy is the establishment of an emotional trust fund upon which we feel we
can draw safely for the rest of our days. If a man breaks
a physical union, we feel he has also broken the emotional one. The market has crashed. The trust fund is
empty. The intimacy that is so central to our existence
has vanished. We are emotionally bankrupt, frighten-
ingly alone.

What do men want? Men, too, want and need intimate relationships. It's just that they see them through
very different lenses than ours. "A relationship is vital to
most men, but it is the central theme for most wom-
en's lives, and I believe the majority of members of both
sexes would agree with that assessment," says a Manhattan psychoanalyst.

A vast divergence exists between men and women in
the realm of intimacy, relationships, and monogamy.
When you talk to hundreds of men, you realize just how
differently the opposite sex thinks, feels, and fantasizes about relationships, love, sex, and monogamy.
Both men and women give lip service to the idea that
the genders are very disparate in these areas, but in actual relationships we often tend to blithely ignore this
vital fact because we like to believe that our partners
think and act exactly the way we do. But, as all my

interviews attest, men are very, very different from you and me.

Sex is perhaps the clearest example of this cleft in male/female thinking. Traditionally for men, sex meant challenge, conquest, and a variety of women. For a woman, sex meant intimacy, belonging, and security. A spate of surveys indicates this division still holds true today. Traditional values have not changed. The attitudes about sex translate into two separate equations.

For most men

Sex equals sex plus sometimes love.

For most women

Sex equals love.

Suzanne, a twenty-two-year-old manicurist from Carlsbad, California, sums it up when she says, "I believe in love. If you're going to be with someone sexually, it's love and he shouldn't be with anyone else. I don't believe my boyfriend could ever be with another woman in bed and also love me."

Her boyfriend, she added reluctantly, disagrees.

Intimacy is another prime example in which males and females branch out in opposing directions. Men differ from women in the amount or degree of emotional intimacy that they expect from each other, according to Dr. Ted Huston, a psychologist at the University of Texas at Austin, who has studied 130 couples intensively. His findings were reported in *The New York Times* (April 1, 1986). Women, Dr. Huston found, expect more intimacy and are gravely disappointed when they don't get it.

In addition, men are confused about what intimacy really is because they have had very little practice in connection on a deep emotional level. The "average" man feels he is relating to a woman through external responsibilities. Very often men consider doing chores or sharing activities as an immersion in intimacy. We love and appreciate having the dishes washed, but this is a far cry from the kind of emotional connectedness that women crave and need.

A third significant area of male/female divergence lies in what each of the sexes finds meaningful and significant in a relationship. Dr. Robert Sternberg, a well-known psychologist at Yale, has studied a group of men and women from seventeen to sixty-nine years old, some of whom have been married for as long as thirty-six years. His conclusions were also reported in *The New York Times* (April 1, 1986), and show marked differences between the sexes in what was important to them in their intimate relationships.

Women rated *fidelity* and *ties to family and friends* as most important in their marriages, while men listed a *wife's ability to make love* and *the couple's shared interests* as priorities.

In short: Monogamy was number one to women, sex was number one to men.

Why do men and women see the world from such different perspectives? In particular, why are intimacy and monogamy so natural for most women and so difficult for a majority of men?

Current psychological thinking that is based largely on Carol Gilligan's brilliant work at Harvard over the last decade has it that a girl's earliest experiences lead her to *connection* with others while a boy's direct him to *independence and autonomy*. In her book, *In a Different Voice* (Harvard University Press, 1982), Gilligan explains that as she matures, a girl must learn to detach just as a boy must be educated to connect. Thus, *as adults, women find themselves uncomfortable with separateness while men are wary of intimacy.*

This female need-for-connectedness and the male need-for-separateness theory is, I believe, the most basic element in the drama of the development of the differences between males and females in the significant areas of their lives. But other factors can play leading roles as I found out from thoughtful men I interviewed.

A high-profile cosmetics executive who specializes in marketing fragrances to women is given to introspection about the strife between men and women. He makes this cogent observation: "Most men grow up in a sports atmosphere. This submerges their individual needs and desires and subordinates them to the team. Most of the metaphors in business are about sports and keep women at a distance. It's easier for a man to deal in a group situation—or to be totally alone—rather than be intimate and monogamous." However, he adds, "Today girls are on the teams, so that there's hope they can be treated more as equals and that this will help them to understand the 'traditional' male mentality of competition and conquest and will make it easier for both sexes to close an undeniable gap."

"My own experience of women," observes a man who is thirty-seven and has had a monogamous marriage for six years, "is that they're incredibly afraid of their own sexuality. Monogamy must be more intense and more important for them. If a woman really lets go, she usually needs to do it in a monogamous situation, whereas a man can experience sexual abandon with a total stranger. I do believe men and women see sexual relationships from two sides of a wide river. What she needs in order to cross that river is love, and for him the bridge is sex."

A research assistant in clinical psychology asserts it is logically very difficult for men to be monogamous. "If one of my primary masculine acts is separation," he pointed out as we discussed Carol Gilligan's ideas, "then it's going to be very hard for me to attach—especially to one woman."

These few remarks give an idea of the kind of think-

ing that I heard from men about relationships and monogamy. For the vast majority of women, monogamy is
essential; it is a deep and abiding need for our sense
of security and well-being in a relationship.

Men aren't against monogamy or intimacy; it's just that
they perceive these aspects of life in a very different
style. When you read what men say about monogamy
in the next chapter, you'll begin to see exactly how uncomfortable and confusing the subject is for them.

THREE

"Monogamy? Is That a Kind of Wood?" He Asked

Webster's defines monogamy as "The state or custom of being married to one person at a time," but the vast majority of women believe that monogamy means

NO PLAYING AROUND—EVER.

Men, on the other hand, have a rainbow of rejoinders to "Tell me what you think monogamy is." I think the fact that there are so many varied hues and tones to the definitions underscores the apparent confusion, anxiety, and unease that the topic engenders among men.

"Let's start out by giving a definition of monogamy," is the way I began interviews because I realized men's notions of the subject were far different from mine, "but don't think about it too long. There's no right or wrong answer. Just tell me what you feel it is, or give me an image of what it is."

"A monogamous relationship is what you *don't* do

rather than what you do do," is the way a twenty-nine-year-old San Diego TV cameraman put it. "Monogamy is *limiting* one's sexual activity to a single partner," explained another man from San Diego who is forty-two and works at the same TV station. "One enters into monogamy to *prevent problems* rather than for a positive benefit," asserts a real estate broker in Annapolis. "Monogamy is a *sacrifice*," echoes a Detroit man. "Monogamy is a *no-win situation*," suggests a psychotherapist who was speaking about his personal beliefs, "it's an *unresolvable issue*. If you stay monogamous, the price you pay is a constant battle with your own impulses." "Monogamy is *obligatory* sex under the nuclear umbrella," says a smart stand-up comic from New York.

The italics in the above definitions are mine. These men see monogamy as a situation that is difficult and requires discipline and restraint.

Other men see it as selfish—in a positive way. "I don't see monogamy as saintly," says a salesman from New York, "I see it as selfish and pragmatic. You're covering your own ass and protecting something that's good." "Monogamy is really for your own benefit," echoes a high school principal from Chicago, "it's a kind of gift to your partner, but ultimately it's for your own good."

Many men, feeling monogamy as oppressive and restrictive, but wanting to please their mates with their fidelity, define it in ways that assure that the ties that bind will do so quite loosely.

A Denver psychotherapist described the it-doesn't-count-if-you-don't-do-it-much syndrome this way. "A man who has a one-nighter or 'affairettes'—more than a weekend but less than an emotional commitment—has a qualified monogamy, which," he concedes, "to a woman means nothing."

He's absolutely correct. "Basically monogamous" is

oxymoronic to females. A woman who discovers that her husband has been unfaithful is not going to be comforted by the knowledge that it was a late-night quickie with a woman whose name he can't remember.

"At Twenty You're a Gland"

Does a man's attitude about monogamy change at various stages and ages of his life? "At twenty you're a gland," explains a man who is now fifty-five, "you just want to get it all the time. That's the way I was until I married at twenty-six. I was monogamous for four years and then the hormones raged again—for two reasons. One, because I have a very strong sex drive, and two, the marriage was bad."

"Up to forty you're ruled by your cock," explains a forty-two-year-old man who also "plays around." "My thinking process now fights for control, but it all starts down there."

On the other hand, almost half of those I interviewed claimed that they have been monogamous, even in their twenties. "To me it's a natural thing to be faithful," says one of these men, a thirty-one-year-old computer salesman, "I require it of a woman and I expect she'll require it of me. I lived with a woman for six years, from the time I was twenty-four until last year. I'm extremely interested in sex, but I was totally monogamous."

The time for temptation is certainly biologically intense in a man's teens and twenties, but however he evaluates his sex drive (usually it's "well above average"), I came to the conclusion that monogamy has to do not with age but with attitude and fulfillment of certain emotional and sexual needs.

The Tournament Species

For my purposes I was primarily interested in why some men are monogamous and others are not, but that doesn't mean I wasn't aware that women—in ever-increasing numbers—stray as well. Men know this, of course, and most will readily admit that they still hold to the double standard. As Robert Sternberg writes of one of his most recent studies on close relationships in *The Triangle of Love* (Basic Books, 1988), "The results clearly showed that men believe that sexual fidelity *is* important—for women."

"Although basically I'm a monogamous guy, and, of course, I expect my wife to be absolutely faithful," said one man with an ironic tone, "I've been programmed to think it's okay for me to have a little on the side. Everybody says that today women are cheating like crazy, but that doesn't change my basic attitude." His thinking resonated with that of most men I interviewed: We know women play around, but we choose not to pay too much attention to that fact and continue on the premise that it is man's inalienable right to sample sexual variety.

Some experts concur with this notion. The English anthropologist Donald Symons writes in *The Evolution of Human Sexuality* (Oxford Press, 1979), that, for evolutionary reasons, men are polygamous and women are not so. In order to propagate the species and spread the gene pool, men become "harem-builders" while women, to protect that gene pool and make sure it survives, are very careful about their sexual alliances.

Sociobiologist David Buss of the University of Michigan also espouses evolutionary theory in an article in *The Psychology of Love* (Yale University Press, 1988), but he uses it to explain *fidelity*. Females of many species, he argues, fend off other females so that they can insure that their offspring will not be deprived of the male's resources. The male, conversely, has a vested interest in guarding the female from participating in other erotic dalliances because it would delay her pregnancy by himself. Thus, if you follow this line of reasoning, you'll see that fidelity fits neatly into the evolutionary framework.

But Professor Buss's theorizing has not yet caught on, either in America or elsewhere. In Zambia, for example, a recent case arose of a jealous wife who caused "grievous bodily harm" to her husband for fooling around with other women. Judge Matthew Chaila informed the housewife, as well as females in general, that "a Zambian man is inherently, culturally and instinctively polygamous and married women who failed to appreciate this fact ran the risk of being plagued by stomach ulcers, high blood pressure, insomnia and alcoholism." This piece of news ran in the Health section in *The Washington Post* (May 24, 1988).

Here in the United States, Beryl Lieff Benderly, in *The Myth of Two Minds: What Gender Means and Doesn't Mean* (Doubleday, 1987), makes some interesting analogies to contemporary males in the animal kingdom. She writes that "some creatures are enthusiastic playboys (technically known as 'tournament species.') They don't form durable bonds with females, but simply 'score' and certain individuals rack up considerably higher scores than others. In extreme cases, as among elephant seals, a small number of heavy hitters can account for half, even three quarters, of the copulations in their neighborhood during an entire breeding season."

But Benderly also writes that while these busy birds and beasts "dance, sing, cavort through the air—whatever is their own species' way of showing off beauty and agility to best advantage, in order to attract as many females as possible, other creatures in nature prefer a happy and monogamous home life."

FOUR

Men Who Stay, Men Who Stray

A woman from San Diego told me, "I had always believed that monogamy was a decision that one made, or a condition that one entered into, and that—demanding or facile as it might be—was that." Many women share her belief. Few of us are aware of the strength needed for navigating the Scylla of desire and Charybdis of lust. I'd never thought much about it myself: I naively assumed that the monogamous man just said NO to temptation or he gave out vibes that he wasn't interested in any messing around. A man named Jeff Frantzen recounted the following experience that showed just how simplistic that notion was.

"Christine was home with the flu," he said, "and we both decided I should go alone to a large cocktail party that good friends of ours were giving. I had a couple of scotches and was about to leave when a very cute girl—cute woman, I should say—came over and started talking with me. I could see she'd had a bit too much to drink, but what she was saying was extremely interesting. She told me what a great blow job she gave, and she wanted me to go home with her. It was hard to walk away from that, but I did. I thought about it often over the following days, and seven years later, I still think about what it would have been like. It was a very conscious decision: I'm married, I'm monogamous, I don't *need* this. But it was not easy."

"You can fall in love with someone else," says the president of a large eastern university, "but it's a very deliberate thing not to allow it. You don't put yourself in a position to fall in love. I strongly believe that any level of infidelity—even one lapse—cannot help but detract from the communication you have with your wife. It harms your relationship even if she never knows about it."

Wimp or Wonderful

Men themselves have very contradictory views of "the monogamous man." Basically male convictions fall into two categories: He's to be respected and even envied, or he's a poor spineless wimp. I recently came across a magazine article that makes the latter point nicely. In an article entitled "The Secret Life of Men" (*Harper's Bazaar*, February 1988), Sean Kelly mocks the monogamous man in this manner: ". . . [He's] an unvirile pill, a loveless leftover on the shelf, an unexciting creep for which his only beloved is being asked to settle. Bad news."

One of the men I interviewed, when asked to give a brief profile of a monogamous man seriously states: "Unromantic. Not very interested in sex. Not very adventurous."

Another observes, "Constricted and fearful."

And still another man says dryly, "Conventional, traditional values, not risk-takers, scared, probably kind of boring when you get right down to it."

Monogamous men are keenly aware that fidelity is often viewed—by other men—as a frailty rather than as a strength. "Yes, there is sexual jealousy when I hear friends talking about all the women they've screwed and I haven't," says an insurance salesman from Palm Beach, Florida, "I don't discuss the fact that I've never made it with another woman other than my wife—with even my closest friend."

"When men talk about sex it sounds the same as 'What restaurant did you eat in last night?' 'Was the food good?' I grew up in that kind of atmosphere, and it didn't hit me that this was a complete devaluation of something that's very important to me until I was an adult. I'm monogamous, but I don't talk about it because it would be misunderstood," says another man who has been married for six years.

"I know what love is now. And I don't want to mess around," says a store owner in Los Angeles. "But other guys put all that pressure on you—like they want you out jamming chicks and cheating on your woman—and talking about all the leg they're getting—that's the dialogue—with their wives in the kitchen cooking dinner and the kids playing on their knee, and they're pulling out pictures of their girlfriends. And it makes them uptight that I'm in love and I'm not playing. So I hang out with myself because I don't like where most men are coming from."

It takes a pretty secure male to admit he adheres to a value that is often derided. So most men who are monogamous don't acknowledge or discuss their singular way with fellow men—they usually shun the subject or stay clear of locker rooms. Men rarely advertise their monogamy except in the Personals columns where women are very much attracted to the word. Traditional values and, of course, the marriage ceremony itself champion monogamy, but when it's man-to-man, "the score" is often what counts most. You can begin to see why it's not so easy to be a monogamous man.

Two Kinds of Monogamy

Since the so-called sexual revolution of the late sixties and early seventies, a great many men and women have had abundant and varied sex lives. This is the first time in our history that a large group of Americans are able to make comparisons between different sexual partners. In other words, both men and women today are aware that one lover may be better than another because we're more sexually experienced than our forebears. A man can be more easily tempted when a strain arises in his relationship because he *knows* there's terrific sex out there waiting to be had. This obviously puts an additional burden on monogamy. Thus, there are really two forms of monogamy, the first has to do with *desire*, the second with *decision*.

The first kind of monogamy is characteristic of the time of infatuation and dazzlement when staying on the straight and narrow comes effortlessly.

The second kind of monogamy is when you consciously decide to uphold a sexual commitment to one person.

During the early stages of a relationship, most men naturally don sexual blinders. "I'd check out other women, it's a knee-jerk reflex," says one man who describes the two kinds of monogamy, "but I just wasn't interested in sex with anybody else. Then a time came when a woman made it clear she was interested in more than mere flirtation. I had to work it out in my mind before I passed on her, whereas a year before, I wouldn't have given the idea more than a passing thought." The second kind of monogamy, which this man describes as working it out "in his mind" is, of course, the more demanding; it requires a deliberate decision to refrain from an experience that he knows to be pleasurable and gratifying.

"At first you both want monogamy," says a gynecologist from Chicago, "and then there's inevitable yearnings and lustings for someone else. At least there was for me, but you can have a desire for someone other than your wife—even if it's a patient—and leave it at that. You can't suppress the desire, you just don't act on it. . . . Questions come into a relationship when it's non-monogamous, and with them, a sense of self-doubt. You're measured and compared. All the beneficial things in a monogamous relationship can't exist in that atmosphere of uncertainty and secrecy. Obviously, I see a great many attractive women in the most intimate way, but I made a vow to be monogamous and that's what I am."

Three Breeds of Monogamous Men

Just as there are two kinds of monogamy, that of unilateral desire and that of deliberate decision, there are three breeds of monogamous men.

The first is the man who accepts monogamy as an ideal and feels it is a principle to which he is committed. Religious values and a parental model are usually the basis for his staunch belief, as is the case with the man quoted just above.

The second kind of monogamous man is the thoughtful, introspective one who has developed his own ideas about what a relationship means to him. For him, fidelity is one of the foundations of an intimate involvement. This man stays dedicated to his conviction of monogamy throughout the course of a long-term liaison or marriage, even if that marriage is breaking up. "I respected my ex-wife and didn't cheat on her ever," says a thirty-nine-year-old litigation lawyer in New York. "There's a level of responsibility to another person, even if it's not working out. She was a good person, and instead of going out to screw, I knew it was time to leave. . . . If you're unfaithful, you're taking something good and twisting it; if what you have is not good, you have to muster the courage to get out."

Another man felt this way: "I'm very sexual and very attracted to other women and I've always seen monogamy as an impossibility. But I don't want to hurt Nancy, my girlfriend, by fucking around. I decided that the only way I could be monogamous was to become friends with a woman, best friends. Nancy and I are the closest friends. I would never screw up a friendship; so when I'm turned on by a woman and want to get it on with her, I think of how much it would ruin the relationship that I have and value. I've thought a lot about this and even though monogamy is really difficult for me, I don't fuck around."

"I've been married twenty-seven years," says an automobile dealer in Boise, Idaho. "My wife has helped me through the good times and the bad. There's a word I believe in: loyalty. I am loyal and I am faithful and I am proud of it. It doesn't mean I don't look at other women and I don't have daydreams. I believe in a spiritual closeness with my wife that could never be violated physically."

The third type of monogamous man elects monogamy—and sticks with it—because the woman he's with has made it possible for him to do so by understanding what he needs physically, emotionally, and intellectually.

Jeff Frantzen, the man quoted at the beginning of this chapter, who still remembers the promise of the ultimate blow job, is one of these. He was "very non-monogamous" during his first marriage. But he has been faith-

ful for seven years in a second marriage and believes he
will continue to stay monogamous "no matter how tur-
bulent it might become." He says he feels that he and
his wife have learned how to weather his (and, also,
her) temptations together.

The first two types of monogamous men, religious ide-
alist and thoughtful adherent, are in the minority. Jeff
and many men like him comprise the third and largest
group of monogamists. "She knows me and knows what
I need, she knows I may feel lust and longing for someone else, and she knows exactly how to deal with me
so that it would never become a problem for us," he says.

BOB SIMONS

I was in my office one morning when I received a call
from a Bob Simons in Philadelphia. He was, he explained, a writer/journalist working on an article with
which I might be able to help him. Would I have a few
minutes to talk? Of course, I said.

He fired some questions at me and, at one point, I re-
joined with, "You know this is tough for me, I'm usually the one doing the asking." As we continued to talk
for a few more minutes, I developed a strong hunch
that Bob Simons would make a good interview himself.

I outlined my subject and he agreed to meet with me
when he was next in New York. I hung up the phone
knowing one single fact about Bob Simons: He was a
writer. I had no idea whether he was married or single, young or old, articulate or not; I just had a notion
that he would have some interesting things to say. And
he did.

New York had come to a virtual standstill the day we
were to talk together. Our office closed early because
of a snowstorm, and I never expected Bob would make
it. But at the appointed hour, four-thirty, a man showed
up at my door.

He smiled, shook off the icy water from his plaid-lined trenchcoat as he took it off, and sat down across from me at the circular table at which I work. He was about thirty, tall, pleasant looking, and a little guarded, or perhaps it was the acquired reserve of a reporter.

We chatted for a couple of minutes about being uncomfortable answering questions when you're used to asking them and I said, "Why don't I get some background? I don't know a thing about you."

Born in Delaware, now living in Philadelphia, a freelance writer, not married, thirty-two years old, living with a girlfriend for the last four years. Had lived with one other woman, and that relationship had lasted three years.

"So let's talk about monogamy," I said, wanting to see where he'd go with the subject without my leading.

"I'm de facto monogamous," he began. "I have an understanding with my girlfriend. I once said that the beginning is the most important part of a relationship. She told me, 'You're crazy, it's the middle, you don't have to go through all those first things. A person is much more interesting when you watch them develop.' "

"Do you both talk about monogamy?" I asked.

"It's an ongoing discussion," he replied. "I'm open about my feelings on this. Monogamy is a negative image to me. I tell her that I can't conceive of never going to bed with another person again. It's continually an issue between us. The subject comes up all the time. I let her know when I'm lusting after somebody. Maybe it's purely idle or maybe there's a hostile element to it. Partly it's blowing off steam. We both see relationships everywhere around us and we discuss them. Monogamy is part of it. I say the idea of monogamy is oppressive to me, yet I'm monogamous."

"And what does she say when you tell her you don't like the concept of monogamy?"

"She says, 'Who's keeping you from screwing around?' Despite her protestations I'm sure she'd be very upset if I did anything about it. If the opportunity arises, I will say to myself her policy is 'Okay, who's stopping you?' and I can go on with it because she's given me permission to do so. I've had occasions when the opportunity was there and didn't follow up. These are generally women I meet in a work environment."

"So, why didn't you follow up?" I responded.

"I guess I can conceive of it if the circumstances were right. I don't know if I'd ever do it even then. But it would have to be a situation where the emotional ramifications are reduced, where the zipless quotient is up. I realize I can fall in love with someone else and I don't want to."

"Do you think you might be faithful simply because your girlfriend isn't holding on tightly to you?"

"Probably so." He stopped to think for a few moments before adding, "Her 'policy' allows me to do what I want whether she means it or not. In giving me that, I love and respect her more—and it reinforces the fact that I don't want to screw up what I have."

"What about marriage, do you think you'll marry your girlfriend?" I asked, switching the subject slightly. I thought he might dodge the question.

"I have a certain opposition to the idea of marriage," he replied, after some more thinking. "I'm a nonconformist to a degree—and a romantic. I have a D. H. Lawrence-y idea about not being restrained or trapped by norms. At a certain point we'd have a common-law marriage. She hints that she'd like to be married, but the big reason for marriage is children. Right now I don't want them. I tell her if you're looking for children, I'm not the guy."

"Then you see marriage as a kind of trap?" I asked.

"Restraint would be better," he responded with a smile.

"But it's still negative, you think of it negatively?" I pursued.

"I always assumed she wanted to nest," he replied detouring the issue, "I assumed she wants marriage. She surprises me by not pushing. She surprises me by being open to my weirder impulses like being a nonconformist and telling me what's stopping me about screwing around. It makes me much more uninhibited and closer to her. There's a good chance that I'll marry her."

"Have you ever wondered if she's been unfaithful?"

"I assume she's monogamous. I like it when she has flirtations. A couple of times it's crossed my mind she's gotten it on with someone. I felt a little shockwave, but it's something hypothetical. At times I take her love for granted. I'm more confident of her love for me than she is of mine for her. At times there's a radical disequilibrium in the power balance in this relationship. Part of it has to do with male/female roles and part with our work. My work is in demand now."

"What does she do?"

"An architect. But she doesn't have the innate sense of confidence or satisfaction that I get from my work because she hasn't had the regular assurances I do of being in demand. She always tells me how terrific I am, but I want more than anything else that she be successful."

The warmth with which he said that made me feel good. I sat back and looked out at the icy snow spattering the window of my office. He was silent too.

Finally, I said, "Tell me about temptation."

"I've had a couple of 'chemical situations' in the last two months," he responded. "I felt attracted to a woman who is much younger. I feel I'd be trifling with her. This is not being immodest, but I can tell she'd fall for me. Even though she'd protest she would—"

"Those are the emotional ramifications you talked about earlier," I added.

"Yes," he said. "I don't want to risk an emotional involvement. The other situation is someone who is more
of a peer. I haven't broached it and won't. It would de-
stroy my relationship with her as a colleague. I now flirt
more and sublimate the sexual influence. I realize there
is a devastating power in sexuality. . . . When I was
younger I felt I had to prove myself sexually. I have a
very strong sex drive."

"How do you deal with that sex drive?"

"Flirtation can be satisfying," he responded. "It is non-
disruptive. You can know someone wants to sleep with
you and you don't follow through. It's in flirtation that
I've gotten some ego gratification. I used to wonder, Am
I attractive? Am I sexually attractive? I can get partial re-
minders from flirtation even though the joy of taking
someone's clothes off whom I've never gone to bed with
is not there. People are dishes on a long table. You want
to sample them. That's still a very appealing model to
me. . . .

"I think, Jesus, life is full of these compromises. I can't
go to bed with that person now. . . . My self-definition
was as a great lover, number one, and as a writer, number two. To have the lover part drop out is an adjustment."

He stopped again. Even though his tone of voice had
not changed, it was clear that this switch of image had
cost him a great deal of hard work.

"What about monogamous sex? Is it good?" I asked.

"It varies. It can be great, good, and not-so-great. But
having had a lot of especially intimate sex for the last
four years, I'd be more rueful now about a wham-bam."

He looked out into the distance. The windows of adja-
cent office buildings were cuffed with white, and down
below, the snow was choking Manhattan. It was time to
wind up the discussion or he would miss his train to
Philadelphia.

"What more can you say about monogamy?" I said, "Anything you want to add? Or take back?"

"Commitment, learning about people, these are my values," he answered, "I used to dismiss the middle period of a relationship in favor of the infatuation and 'firsts.' My girlfriend changes and develops and I love to watch this and be involved with it. The big change for me is that I used to be so intrigued when a woman took off her clothes, but I realize now there are only so many times that's exciting. The sex part is still *very important* to me. The richness of Susan's intimate life and of our life as it unfolds is fascinating. Screwing around is a vain exercise."

WHAT KEEPS HIM MONOGAMOUS

The reason I've excerpted Bob Simons's interview at such length is that, D. H. Lawrence-y nonconformist/ romantic as he may be, he's hit upon most points—both positive and negative—that are important to know about monogamous men. These are the key words/phrases to keep in mind:

- I can't conceive of never going to bed with another person again.
- Okay, who's stopping you?
- I tell her I'm lusting after somebody.
- She always tells me how terrific I am.
- Flirtation.
- I have a strong sex drive.
- Sex is *very important* to me.
- There is a devastating power in sexuality. . . .

"I can't conceive of never going to bed with another person again." Confronted with *never*, most of us have one

of two reactions: rebellion or depression. Monogamy does mean never being unfaithful, but for most men, the concept is supremely difficult to embrace. A Los Angeles television executive who is very attractive to women and very much attracted to them is thoroughly monogamous, but he allows himself psychological space to move in so that he doesn't feel trapped by the full impact of "never." "If you find someone to whom you make a commitment, you have to leave a little escape valve," he says. "It's like the bottle of booze or a pack of cigarettes for smokers who've given it up. Monogamy has got to be that you *want* to rather than you *have* to."

Another man adds to the smoking example, "I'd consciously fight the idea that I couldn't have a cigarette, and then want one all the more. The more pronouncements you make to yourself about monogamy, the more you feel you can never have another woman, the more you feel you have to, and that's when you begin to fuck around."

The idea of an escape valve is central here. A man needs to feel that *he can act* on his desires and that *he chooses not to*. A thirty-four-year-old man, monogamous, married for eight years, says directly, "I'd suffocate sexually unless I tell myself that a great screw is still a possibility in my life."

"Okay, who's stopping you?" Part of the crucial escape valve for a monogamous man can be provided by his wife or lover. A woman who says, in effect, go ahead, as did Bob Simons's girlfriend, gives him a feeling of sexual relief while at the same time reinforcing the bond between them. The idea is an old one: In letting someone go, you're more likely to keep him.

I spoke with a woman, a commercial banker, whose attitude was the same as Bob Simons's girlfriend. She has been married to another banker for six years, and the marriage is monogamous on both sides. "I'm not sure whether I mean it or not when I say to John that I would understand if he had a one-night fling. He travels, he gets lonely, I'm often not available because I'm away on business too. Reason tells me that it might happen—to either one of us—and that it wouldn't alter our marriage, which we both consider paramount. I'm sure that because he has an escape hatch, he feels more comfortable, but I probably would freak out if it ever did happen. I just instinctively know he needs to believe he's not locked in." She, on the other hand, likes the "locked-in" feeling. "He tells me he'd go crazy if I ever was unfaithful. He's done everything including making me swear on a Bible that I'd never go to bed with another man, and that feels good to me."

"I tell her I'm lusting after somebody." Many men that I interviewed told their partners when they were attracted to another woman. "By telling Elizabeth that I think so-and-so was hot, it somehow insures that I won't act on my impulses," said one man.

"It would also tend to make Elizabeth jealous, wouldn't it?" I asked.

"That's just the point. She gets a little bothered by it, and the sex that night is different. It somehow has an added dimension to it. The other woman makes her competitive and she pays more attention to me. She tells me when she thinks a guy is attractive, and I have the same reaction. I like to know that other men find her sexy. We talk about this a great deal. I think it's one of the reasons we continued to have such an intense sex life after nine years."

Talking about who turns him on and who doesn't is one of the ways a monogamous man defuses the sexual fireworks that inevitably go off for him from time to time. Instead of being threatened by these sexual missiles that he's firing off, the psychologically sensitive woman understands them and is, in return, rewarded by a deeper and richer intimacy with her mate.

A Manhattan therapist underscores this important point: "Couples," he says, "who do not express their sexual interest in others and who repress those feelings are in a more precarious position. It's harmless to want or to wish. Not being able to say what you fantasize about pushes you even more to act out those fantasies and impulses."

"She always tells me how terrific I am." When Bob Simons's girlfriend tells him his writing is powerful or his looks are appealing or his prowess as a lover is sensational, she's practicing *reinforcement*, a cardinal tenet of the psychological canon.

The premise of the reinforcement theory is that if you compliment someone on something that matters to him—work, looks, talent, sex, for example—the chances are that that person will like you more. What Susan achieves by telling Bob he's "terrific" is to continuously increase his attraction—and attachment—to her.

"Flirtation." "I'm monogamous, but I couldn't live without some sexual connection with other women. I guess you could best describe it as flirting," says an extremely sexy man. Life, he says, has no zest without flirting. "Flirting is the paprika of existence. Eye-lock, the sexy smile, the brushing touch on the arm—it makes you feel good. It makes you a sexual being outside of the being that you are with your wife."

Flirtation is another way of bolstering a sagging ego—and breathes there a man (or woman) who has never needed this? A seductive look, an appreciative side-glance, a brushing touch on the arm, can set you up for the rest of the day. "A marriage can't be open," says a writer

friend of mine from Maine, "but it has to be porous."
For monogamous men—and women—flirtation stretches
the fibers of a relationship but keeps it intact.

"I have a strong sex drive. Sex is very important to me."
I mentioned previously that with only two or three exceptions, every single one of the men that I interviewed
reported that they had "strong," "above average," or
"high" sex drives.

Throughout his entire life, a man conceives of himself
as a sexual being. The fact of his penis's existence and
its behavior is never far from his conscious mind. Although this may seem extremely obvious, most women
are not cognizant of this or if we are, it seems to slip our
minds. A man, however, never forgets. His response
to his own sexuality is constant, consistent, and lifelong.
"A man and his penis are one, a woman and her va-
gina separate with ease," said one of the men I talked
with. The majority of males would agree with him.

One's masculinity is often assessed by his peers by how
many women he's made it with, points out a psychotherapist I spoke with. "For many men," he says, "the
concept of self, his identity, is inextricably involved with
the penis. Sexuality is not a woman's total identity. She
is more bound up with security; sexuality is not her concept of herself as a woman."

The monogamous man is as sexual as a non-monogamous one. He is constantly aware of sexual possibilities; he needs to feel he is a romantic pursuer; his
hormones buzz when a desirable woman crosses his
path; he fantasizes about the exquisitely pleasurable moment of seeing her body naked for the first time; he
imagines tousled sheets, the intimate sounds that she
makes.

Says a sage male psychiatrist, "Women must always
remember that men need to feel that they are the best

lovers in the world." This notion is exemplified by Bob Simons. He had always perceived himself as a lover first, and professional second—and a great many men, both monogamous and not, define themselves in precisely the same way.

"There is a devastating power in sexuality . . ." All men think sex is important, but monogamous men believe that sexuality has a devastating power in two areas—love and trust.

"I once had a one-nighter," a man admitted reluctantly, "and it set off alarms for me. It felt good. I wanted more. I had to cut out screwing around right at the start because once I got into it, I felt I wouldn't be able to stop. And I realized that it could lead to the end of my marriage because I could fall in love. I think about that woman; I know where she lives even now. I even remember her number because I've picked up the phone to call her—especially if I've had too much to drink or smoked a joint. But I've never been unfaithful except that once, and it's been eleven years."

A man and his feelings are only one half of the equation of infidelity. The other half lies with the other woman. She can even more easily fall in love with him than he with her because she typically measures sex in terms of love. A woman who believes she's in love with a man can present him with the most potent kind of emotional snare, one that can make it extremely difficult to extricate himself.

One of the monogamous men I interviewed tells of this searing experience with a woman who had fallen in love with him: "I'd always wanted a close female friend," he recounted, "and Margie filled the bill. She was my business partner, she and my wife were pals, she loved my kids, she knew all my good points and tolerated the bad. We'd gone to bed together once before I was married—and we had hashed it over that we'd never do it together again, it was just one of those things. . . . We were in the office having lunch one day—I remember clearly that she was stirring milk into a container of coffee—and she said 'I'm in love with you, Doug. I've been in love with you since that night.'

"We always had a lot of laughs together. My first reaction was that she was putting me on. But she wasn't joking. 'That night' had been four years ago, and both she and I had been married since then and we each had two kids! It had been nothing more than friendly sex for me. And of course I thought it was the same for her.

"She wanted to sleep with me again. She wanted *me* so badly that I wanted her too. I loved Ellen, my wife—and I've never been unfaithful. But the pressure was horrible.

"Margie would see me every day and, even though she tried not to say anything, it was always there between us. Finally, I thought I'd go nuts if it went on any longer. I told my wife what had happened and I decided to break up the business partnership with Margie. The cost of one summer night of good sex between buddies was inestimable. I'll never be the same again."

Falling in love can be one of the catastrophic fallouts of infidelity but although it's not inevitable, another devastating phenomenon does invariably occur—the breaking of trust. Monogamous men mentioned this again and again. Even though their wives or girlfriends might never know about a casual encounter, they said, any sexual dalliance rips apart a bond of trust.

"I think about sleeping with other women especially when I'm away and I'm lonely or we're going through a tough period in the relationship," says a bicoastal executive who maintains apartments in New York and Los Angeles. "But I know I won't be able to look at my wife in the same way, and I'd be betraying the trust I've spent four and a half years to build. Until you know about building that bankroll of trust, you don't realize you really have something to lose."

"What," I asked this man, "happens if you're very lonely or the 'tough period' lasts a long time? How do you deal with this sexually?"

"I masturbate—because I need a lot of sex. And I also sublimate—by getting so involved with work that I can't think of sex. As a last resort, I go to the gym and swim laps until I drop. Then I'll come back to the hotel, jerk off, go to sleep. If I can't sleep, I'll take a sleeping pill. I use them when I travel to Europe, but I keep a couple on hand in case the nights get too long and too lonely. But I will *not* fuck around no matter how bad it gets."

FIVE

Hotel Room, Chicago

What monogamous men say is fascinating as well as instructive, but it's necessary to explore the flip side of the coin. I found that the men who stray reveal much more than the men who stay. They give us an inside look at what went wrong and once you know what, how, and why that may be, you have one more key to understanding how to keep your own relationship monogamous. In this chapter you'll read the words of men who are revealing the most private parts of their lives.

It was on a brilliantly sunny and windy May day that I met Bill Rostoff in a hotel room in Chicago. A friend who knew what I was working on had suggested that my project might benefit from talking with a man who, by his own account, had "fooled around a lot." As it happened, I had met Bill Rostoff very briefly at a gala celebration party that he and his wife had given four or five years before. The party was memorable because it was so beautifully done. I clearly remembered walking into the Rostoffs' home in the Old Town section of Chicago and seeing endless shimmering candles and the soft luster of polished walnut floors, pale beige covered furniture, and lacquered cream walls with an exceptional collection of German expressionist drawings in heavy carved gold frames.

A dozen or so round tables had been placed in the dining room and at one end of the long drawing room. Each was set with a ravishing bouquet of freesia, white roses, white tulips, and lilies of the valley, along with glittering crystal, silver, and antique china. At the other end of the room, a young woman whose long blond hair spilled over the shoulders of her ivory-colored chiffon dress was playing a harp. The atmosphere was knockout: sophisticated, intensely chic. Not the smallest detail was out of whack.

I met Bill's wife, Martha, for only a few moments. She was a tall woman in her late thirties who could have graced the cover of *Town and Country* magazine. Her cool beauty was heightened by her captivating charm and elegant style. As Bill and Martha stood there, both relaxed and self-confident in that glowing room, greeting their guests together, to me, and to everyone who saw them, they were an enviably perfect couple.

Now, several years later, I was in Chicago again and Bill Rostoff was about to arrive at my hotel for an interview on the subject of monogamy.

I had ordered some coffee for us and was stirring sugar into my cup as I looked out over a white-capped Lake Michigan and speculated about Bill. I knew from my colleague that his marriage to Martha was his second and they had three children, a son and two daughters, and that Bill was forty-three. I knew also that he was a very successful electronics entrepreneur and had sold his firm to a large conglomerate not less than a year before.

My speculation about his private life was that he had been non-monogamous during his first marriage and totally faithful to Martha to whom he'd been married for nine years.

At ten sharp he knocked on the door. When I opened it I saw Bill in grey sweatpants and hooded sweatshirt, gym bag in hand, orange windbreaker slung casually over one shoulder, his color high from good health, the wind, and the late spring sun. He walked into the room, dropped his duffle in an easy chair so that he could shake hands, and sat himself on the sofa next to the coffee tray. He was a pleasant-looking man: short sandy hair mingled with gray, clear blue eyes, and the attractive, easy movements of a man whose body is still competitively athletic.

He apologetically asked for tea rather than coffee, and I dialed room service to have some brought up while he settled himself comfortably on the sofa.

He knew the topic, since I'd told him on the phone in general the areas we'd be discussing when we'd made the appointment to meet. I had explained we would need at least two hours.

"I'm sure your time is limited," I began, "so no pre-liminaries. Let's just start unless you have any questions."

"I have several hours, as many as you need," he said affably with an engaging smile. "You heard from Jim that I'm not working since I sold my company. As a matter of fact, I'm not sure what I'm going to do with the rest of my life, so I have as much time as it takes."

"That's great," I said, "so how about defining monogamy for starters? Don't think too much on this one. It doesn't have to be for Webster's."

"Monogamy is a decision," he said after a moment's pause, "one woman at a time. One relationship at a time."

"Now, tell me something about you. I know very little. Where are you from? Where did you go to school? When did you marry? That kind of thing."

"I was born right here on the South Side; my father

was a baker. I was a jock and my family wanted me to go to Northwestern, but I got a full athletic scholarship to a Texas school.

"You want to know about monogamy. Well, I have a basic theory about men and women. Most guys grow up being socially inept with women. In every group there are guys who have looks, know how to dance, but most of us look funny. When I called a girl, I literally made a list of eight things to talk about because what if I didn't know what to say to her?

"I went to school on a football scholarship. Girls were part of the deal. The alumni fixed me up with lots of girls every weekend. I ended up throwing them out on Friday nights or I sold them to fraternity brothers or teachers. The girls didn't know, of course. They were college girls from nearby schools who were known to be friendly."

"Sold the girls? What does that mean?" I asked.

"Well, one went to a teacher for an A in a course. Others went to fraternity brothers because I needed the money. It doesn't sound very good. As a matter of fact, those weren't great times for me. I'd walk by the library and I'd see couples holding hands and I'd be envious. I wanted to be with someone I really liked. So when I met my first wife, who was also a student, I had a feeling that I was saved. I worried that no one would ever love me, that I would become a major degenerate because of all the drinking and fooling around I was doing. You have to understand what it's like to be a major jock at a major athletic school. I never fit in with it. I was lonely.

"I married her because I thought it would save my life. At that time I thought I would stay with sports, be a football player. I felt good with her, not in love, but better than usual. We married when I was twenty-two. I didn't think about fooling around one way or the other when I got married. Monogamy was not a concern."

He turned to the tray with the teapot and poured himself another cup. Then he walked over to the window, looked out for a few moments and returned to his place on the sofa, feet again crossed on the table in front of him.

"So," he looked keenly at me, "it was a year and a half after I was married when a twenty-six-year-old invited me to her apartment. By that time I was back in Chicago, had given up the football, and needed to make a living. I was working at a job developing sales techniques. She worked where I worked and I thought, 'God, I'd better do it before she realizes what's happening, before she stops coming on to me!' I didn't feel guilty. Guilt meant taking time away from my family—I had a child by then—and it usually happened at lunch.

"That started a pattern. I fooled around a lot. I was unhappy about it. I did some locker-room talking with other guys who were doing the same thing and it sounded bad to me. I'd say to myself, 'Never again, I've learned my lesson. It's not what I want.' Then I'd step into the elevator at work, and an interesting girl would get in, and I'd forget what I told myself eight floors above."

Bill shifted his feet and his tone and said, "I can see you have a list of questions for me, but it's easier for me to talk this way. Is it okay with you?"

"Of course," I replied. "As you can imagine, I find your story fascinating and so will other women. As long as you have time, I'm listening very carefully."

I checked my tape recorder while he leaned his head back thoughtfully and continued. "When someone's a stranger to you, it's the difference between reading a play and seeing it. Sometimes reading is better because your imagination gives it more life than it has on the stage. When you know only a small part of someone, your imagination fills in the rest as great. It's the same with having sex with a new person. You always think this woman is going to be different, but it ends up as always the same thing, nothing.

"At one point I was seeing a woman every week at this very hotel. It was between all the business meetings, the pressure, the work. For forty-five minutes I could escape to a room like this and have a sensual time. It was a good way out. She was a physically attractive woman, but if we had to have dinner every week before we went to bed, it would have ended in one week. That lasted a year with a few flings in between here in Chicago and when I was traveling. And then I met someone who made me realize that what I had been looking for was not a body but love. I really fell in love with Martha, my second wife."

He stopped and I waited for him to resume. But he looked out over Lake Michigan, absorbed in some gathering gray clouds and the now white-hooded waves.

"What made Martha so different from all the rest? Why did you fall in love with her?" I asked after a few moments.

"I've always been incredibly tense, and the only time I'm not is when I'm out on the lake sailing alone or with the children. I'm tense because I'm in a rush, pushing on to the next thing, no time to enjoy the present. I find myself attracted to people who are relaxed. Martha was relaxed. Her voice is soft not harsh. She fits visually for me too. I still like seeing her undress after nine years. The chemistry is right."

I remembered Martha Rostoff as I'd seen her the night of their party. Serene and charming with a hundred or more guests at her home for dinner. Bill himself had seemed equally unruffled that evening, although I'd only been around him for a few minutes. Today, too, he seemed as relaxed and casual as a man could be.

"I've always been a high-tension person," he said, tuning into my thoughts, "but in the past year I've begun to try and be easier with myself. Martha gave me a certain sense of tranquillity . . . I love Martha—" he stopped again.

"But I fooled around a lot after I married her, too," he continued, again looking out to the lake. "In the period with Martha I've had four relationships worth remembering. One is a relationship that never happened. I was working until two every morning with a group of people including a young marketing manager. Nothing ever went on between us because she wouldn't allow it, but she was a lot like Martha, easy in a tense situation.

"Then I had a thing with a woman I met in Washington. I saw her at least once a month for two years, and I know she was in love with me. She was kind, considerate, had a wonderful husband, and with her I felt a great deal of guilt because I wasn't completely truthful. I said I stayed married because of my child, but if I'd been honest, I would have said I wouldn't leave Martha. I broke it off because I didn't want to hurt her even more.

"After that I became involved with a knockout of a girl. It was another escape from tension. I went to a therapist when I started seeing her. 'I've got to stop this,' I told him. His attitude shocked me. Basically what he said was stop being so hard on yourself. Look at the boring life we all live, you're seeking adventure and what's so bad about that. I said to myself there's nothing wrong except if you're caught and you lose what you value. If you value your wife and you love her, it's crazy to risk the marriage. I stopped seeing him and stopped fooling around. That was four years ago."

He uncrossed his legs and straightened his shoulders. From his tone, I was almost positive that he would continue and say ". . .and I've been faithful ever since."

"The fourth woman I was involved with," he went on, "was when I sold my company a year ago. Circumstances threw us together and that was it. I wasn't working, my wife was becoming more tied up with the charity work that's a big part of her life now, and it's very time-consuming and stressful for her. I was basically relaxed and Martha would come home tense and concerned about her projects. Even though I completely acknowledge that she's benefiting the community by what she does, I'd be pissed that she brought tension to my world at home. I wanted to change my life. This woman was European, she wanted to live in France, a quiet life. Just what I wanted, a peaceful, easy world of my own. I had terrible conflicts about my children and Martha, but I would have broken it off to have that kind of life. Actually, the woman ended things between us. She met another man at work and married him several months ago."

The sky was now uniformly gray. I switched on the lamp on the end table to give some warmth to the room. We had been talking for almost two hours.

"What's happening now?" I asked.

"The tension at home is driving me crazy. Martha is having the place redecorated. I try and spend as much time as I can on the boat and at the gym. Even though I don't like being alone, it works for me when I sail because it's tranquil and the lake gives me a perspective on life. I keep thinking and hoping that with Martha things will get better every year. If we ever get on the same time clock, things will be terrific. That's why I'm afraid to start another business. I'm waiting."

I wondered whether he was seeing other women.

"Do you think Martha knew about these other involvements?" I asked.

He thought for several moments. "I think she did. I believe she was aware that I fooled around, but she never felt anything serious would come of it. She didn't know of my emotional attachments with the women I mentioned to you. If she had ever realized that there was more to it than sex, I don't know what would have happened. I'm pretty certain she would have left me if she thought it was an involvement.

"You know," he said, again looking intently at me, "you can say you're tense, she was attractive, things happened, but the fact is that you're doing something dishonest and betraying someone who has your trust. I always wanted to keep my word, not to lie. I've never once cheated on a business deal, taken a kickback, and yet in the area that should be the most important of all, I've done it. It's stupid."

"Have you seen anyone else since the European woman?" I asked.

"No, in the last eight months I've been totally monogamous. And I like to think I'm going to stay that way."

"Do you feel you could spend the rest of your life being faithful?"

"I would like to think so. I won't fool around ever again because some woman is great looking. The only way I'll do it is if a woman gets under my skin."

I wasn't clear what he meant by that and was about to ask him when he continued.

"Cross out what I just said. I'm lying to myself. I don't have the will power to walk away from something that really intrigues me. But I'll be home every night. That is certain. I know that my marriage is too important to ever break up. But just before I came here, I saw this terrific-looking woman walking down Michigan Avenue and I said, 'Oh shit, not again.' Thank God she was smoking."

The Womanizer

Men like Bill Rostoff belong to the tournament species. They're often labeled "womanizers." Gary Hart, Marcello Mastroianni, Warren Beatty, Picasso, John Kennedy and his father have been among the more publicized of the type.

Take the case of Gary Hart, for example. Dr. Judd Marmor, a psychoanalyst in Los Angeles who was interviewed by *The New York Times* on Hart's behavior, feels that Hart's womanizing syndrome can be in part attributed to "the seduction of the spirit that takes place when you are surrounded by admiring throngs, when the red carpet is laid out for you."

On a less public stage, this was also the scenario that Bill Rostoff found himself in. "I was becoming more powerful in business," he said. "I looked good in a suit and the twenty-seven-year-olds would say 'God, this guy is smart in a meeting. He's smart and he looks good.' It has to do with power and admiration. And taking risks. And opportunity . . . I know a terrific-looking carpenter in Wisconsin who loves his wife but is dying to get laid. If he had been in publishing or advertising, he wouldn't have been able to avoid it."

Seduction of the spirit and of the body, conquest, risk, adventure, opportunity—these are familiar chapter headings in the womanizer's story. As a character, he's quite consistent whether he is chairman of the board, carpenter, salesman, artist, or computer consultant. But that's only part of the tale. Before you can fully understand the basic psychological profile of this kind of man, listen to these experiences of an introspective and articulate "womanizer."

"I'd enjoy being interviewed," he had said when I asked if he'd talk with me, "because I've thought a lot about monogamy." We agreed to meet in my office in midtown at four on a Wednesday afternoon.

Gerald Terrell has Paul-Newman-blue eyes and a fresh, just-washed feeling about him. He's a good-looking man and, although one senses that he knows it, it doesn't interfere with his intense focus on the person he's talking with—which makes him doubly seductive. At thirty-nine, he's been married for thirteen years and has two sons, nine and eleven. We started the interview by talking about his wife and family and when he first became interested in "the chase."

"There were guys in school that gambled, drank, played football, and there were guys that were into women," he explained. "We were ladies' men—that was our sport. You don't want to give up that talent when you're married . . . I married when I was twenty-six. I'd played around a lot and felt it was time to settle down and have a family. I was monogamous for five years, but it was tough. My first child was almost a year old when it happened. I was working in Dallas in a real estate firm where there were a lot of women. My wife was back East with the baby visiting her parents, and instead of going home to a TV special, I took one of the women who worked with me out to dinner.

"She had suggested we go to a restaurant in a hotel which was nearby. She had planned this entire event—the restaurant, the corner table, everything—down to reserving a room in the hotel itself. She told me jokingly about what she'd done and I said, 'Let's go!' thinking it was a game, and she stood up from the table and we went upstairs. She wanted to get something from it, a relationship, an involvement, a promotion. I was caught up in the physical excitement of the whole scene. I'd had some wine and I woke up with tremendous guilt. I can't tell you how badly I felt. Nothing happened for several months, and then we had an evening again and it was passionate, thrilling. I thought my marriage was strong, but my wife and I didn't have a great sex life. It was the novelty of a new woman. My major concern was getting caught and I didn't, and the marriage wasn't threatened, so the fear and the guilt became less of a problem."

He stopped for a moment before continuing, "One of the major motivations of men who aren't moral is the chase. The chase is probably much more fun than the conquest.

"You see a pretty woman and you say 'I'd like to spend the night with her,' and you start making moves and it's a challenge. There are fifty other guys who have the same feeling. It's like sports or if you want to put it into psychological terms, it's chasing after your mother, the woman you couldn't have. There's a highly competitive zone of action for the woman's attention. You go after her with all the cleverness you can muster. When you succeed, it's terrific, it's a high, it's fun. Once the conquest occurs with this type of guy—a guy like me—the relationship ends because it's no more magic than the last. The race was more important than the finish line. If you don't get to the finish line, you need someone else to assuage your ego. If you got to the finish and won the race, you're high and you seek it again. In the next one, there may be magic. So you keep running, always."

"Did you ever think that with one of these women the magic would materialize, that you'd fall in love?" I asked.

"I never thought about 'love' like that. Love would mean leaving my wife and I wasn't prepared to do that. But it did happen. I did fall in love.

"I worked late one night and took Nancy, my secretary, out for dinner. I realized that night that the person who worried, cared for me, and was there for me even more than my wife was Nancy. My wife was going to graduate school in the evenings and, although she took care of the children and me, somehow she wasn't there. I know it sounds pretty selfish, but I was used to my wife being there. I felt she hadn't given me enough notice that she'd be gone from my life while she was at school. The night I took Nancy out for dinner, I became aware she was more involved in my life than my wife was. I fell in love with her. Really in love. Something I never thought would happen. I was ready to leave my wife, the kids, everything I'd worked for.

"Nancy was ten years younger than I was, she was attracted to power, father image, drive, intelligence, loyalty to the boss. I got great sex, adoration, incredible commitment. So I said to myself, 'I've had enough. I'm tired of the chase, and what I've been chasing I've finally found. I found the magic. I'll make the commitment. Divorce. Monogamy. The whole ball of wax. Even another child'—which Nancy wanted.

"I was in the process of leaving my wife, but these things take time. And during one of those times I was away on business, Nancy found out that I'd been with another woman for the night. It meant nothing to me. I was lonely in a hotel in Detroit and this woman came on to me. It was just sex, another conquest. But Nancy ended it. She told me that she knew what I had done before her, and that I would do it after I married her. And she couldn't take it. She had to have a man who would be faithful."

"And you cannot be faithful? Even with the magical person?" I asked.

"Once a guy plays and is good at it," he responded, "there's a better than fifty-fifty chance he'll do it again. I tried to tell Nancy that I could be monogamous, but she wouldn't buy it and I think she was right."

"After Nancy what happened?"

"I kept playing and I still do. My wife must be aware

at some level. She took me back after the mess with Nancy. She must know what I'm doing, but on a more conscious basis, she shields herself from knowing."

"What if you fall in love again?"

"I'll take my chances. Part of me says it will never happen. Another part of me says if it does, I'll get out of the marriage. I'm playing with fire, but I can't help myself," he flashed a bittersweet grin at me. "The chase, the win—it's too much fun to give up."

To the womanizer—and Gerald Terrell is a pretty articulate example of one—the lure of non-monogamy is absolutely irresistible. This kind of man can be unfaithful within a matter of hours or days, as was the commodities broker I interviewed who waited less than a week to consummate an attraction to one of his wife's bridesmaids. By his own admission, his behavior had a compulsive, repetitive quality. "I couldn't stop myself," he said, and then he added a very significant afterthought, "I just love women."

One of the therapists I interviewed invokes the "wave theory" about womanizers. "He rides the crest from relationship to relationship," the therapist explains. "The newness is a turn-on, it's the crest of the wave. As one wave recedes, he moves on to the next wave. The crests are the highs, the stimulants, that's what gives the behavior its addictive quality."

A well-known New York psychiatrist explains the womanizer's compulsive functioning this way. "When a man repetitively seeks sex with women, he is exhibiting a defense mechanism, he is defending himself against being a nonentity. In spite of his commonsense awareness of the consequences, and the disregard for moral and ethical values, and for the effect it has on the woman, he can't give up his behavior because it's a question of self-preservation."

These men invariably offer rationalizations for their actions. "He feels he's doing it for the pleasure and erotic gratification it gives him," this same psychiatrist explains. "He'll tell you he really likes women, loves sex, that the sex life at home isn't so great. He may say he's competitive and loves to win." Hearing this, I remembered both Gerald Terrell and Bill Rostoff as well as numerous others voicing those exact words.

"They can't explain why they are doing something so dangerous, so they justify it to themselves by saying they're fascinated by women, they have unusually high sex drives, or that their wives are lacking. In effect," the doctor pointed out, "on an unconscious level they disregard and abuse women, but there's also a masochistic quality to the womanizer's behavior. The man can be abused by the woman. Donna Rice abused Hart, for example, and it was *her* friend that blew the whistle on the whole affair."

Today, the psychological community generally views womanizers as sex addicts—men who cannot stop from indulging in sexual affairs, even when the behavior jeopardizes their primary intimate relationship.

From 3 to 6 percent of Americans are sexual addicts according to Dr. Patrick Carnes, a family therapist at the Golden Valley Health Center in Minnesota, author of *Out of the Shadows: Understanding Sexual Addiction* (Compare Publications, 1986). (About 80 percent of those who seek treatment are men, although he suspects more women are afflicted than this statistic suggests.)

Recent research is focusing on the spouses of men who have repeated extramarital affairs. The term for such spouses is *coaddict*. Abandoning the role of the coaddict is often crucial for the recovery of the addict himself. Typically, the wife or lover of a womanizer is so needy that she is willing to settle for almost any mate and then convinces herself that she cannot live without that person. She is usually terrified of abandonment and does anything she can to maintain the relationship, ignoring her own feelings and needs, excusing his behavior and avoiding conflicts and confrontation. As an ironic result, she is helping to perpetuate her mate's behavior. By accepting an unacceptable situation and deliberately sidestepping a showdown, she does nothing to force her partner to acknowledge his addiction and the hurtful consequences of his behavior and seek help.

The prescribed treatment for both the victim of sexual addiction and the coaddict today primarily consists of psychotherapy or marital counseling and attending peer group support meetings that are based on the twelve steps model developed by Alcoholics Anonymous. A recent book, *Back from Betrayal: Recovering from His Affairs* (Harper & Row, 1988), by Jennifer P. Schneider, gives more details on the syndrome of both addict and coaddict and outlines the kinds of help available for both.

SIX

The Long-Term Lover, the One-Night Stander, and the Occasional Strayer

Fortunately the womanizer is a pretty rare breed. Much more common are men who are not compulsively sexual but who "mess around" nevertheless. Males who are not monogamous come in all shapes, sizes, and ages, but most of them topple into one of three different styles of infidelity: the one-night stander, the long-term lover, and the occasional strayer. It does not matter whether a man is married, a live-in lover or a less-than-casual boyfriend—he is still subject to the lures of infidelity. One man I interviewed sums it up this way, "Better dispel the illusion that he'll be faithful once he gets married."

He's right. I found that marriage vows usually don't keep a man monogamous. In the following pages we'll take a look at these three kinds of men who stray and penetrate the motives that underlie their unfaithful behavior.

The One-Night Stander

This man is often away on business; during his travels he will accept the sexual services of a willing and/or attractive woman who offers them at a price—dinner, drinks, or actual money. The one-night stander may also be interested in prostitutes or call girls, but his pursuit of this kind of pleasure has been almost totally diminished because of AIDS.

A one-night stand, as men use the term, is also the equivalent of a sexual quickie: a wham-bam behind closed doors in a private office, an afternoon liaison at a motel or hotel, or a dalliance in the leatherette backseat of a taxi.

Frank Donnelly, a practicing psychotherapist in New York, succinctly explains the one-night stander's behavior in this way, "Basically, he's jerking off with someone else. He is a man who is not relating—there's no work to be done with his partner, no intimacy involved, no demand to connect except on a physical basis. One-night stands are for people who need a certain kind of closeness, and sexual intercourse provides that momentarily. It's like eating whipped cream all the time. It becomes nauseating after a while. But then you crave it again."

The man who has one-night stands with professionals or pays for sex in some manner, according to another therapist, may also be following an established, deeply entrenched cultural mode. "Certain men will seek paid-for sex," he explains, "and certain men don't. Cultural patterning doesn't die easily. Despite the ever-present threat of AIDS, some men feel that the only way they can have extramarital sex is with a professional."

"It was acceptable to go to a prostitute," a man from New Orleans told me. "My father took me to a woman when I was fourteen and told her to teach me. It was a classic situation. . . . I continued to pay visits during my marriage. Still do. An affair is out of the question. My wife probably knows what I've been doing, everyone knows what everyone else does within a certain circle here. AIDS has not stopped me except for the fact that I now always use protection. Where I go, it's also known that the women are considered 'clean'. They are tested regularly, and the use of needles or any kind of drugs is forbidden. That's why the prices are so high."

"The guys went. I went too," explains a man from Queens, New York, who frequented a neighborhood bar where he knew he could pick up a woman for a few dollars and/or a few drinks. "It was about the same as playing basketball together, which we also do every week. The advertising on diseases has done a number on me, though, and I've stopped screwing around like that. Now if a woman is interested, I have to be absolutely positive she's not a professional and I use two condoms. Usually, one of the guys will tell me he's made it with so-and-so and she's got a friend and here's her phone number if I ever want to use it. It's no sweat to take it from there."

A young professor at one of the Ivy League universities who has been in a relationship that's lasted four years said, "I believe in monogamy and I've stuck to it— except for one night. Prostitutes have always held a certain attraction for me. I would always take precautions so AIDS doesn't trouble me, but the political implications of prostitution do. If there were whorehouses for women, I'd feel better. . . . I was on a grant and traveling in the Far East. I hadn't been laid in several weeks and I went to a prostitute. The allure was a new body, a different body. Flesh. Mystery. The whole fantasy of a brothel. I argued about the price. We ended up at three dollars. It was a pretty disappointing experience. I was premature, anxious. Yet I'm still interested in the idea."

"Usually a more educated man won't pick up a prostitute," asserts Dr. Anthony Pietropinto, a psychiatrist and coauthor with Jacqueline Siminauer of *Beyond the Male Myth: What Women Want to Know About Men's Sexuality* (Times Books, 1977). "He'll probably masturbate. There are many men who wouldn't dream of paying for sex ever. Probably about sixty to seventy-five percent of men in what we call the upper classes fall into that category."

One man I interviewed who has been monogamous over a nineteen-year period—except for one night—recounted this experience. "My wife and I have the closest kind of relationship. We have often discussed the possibility of outside sex and have vowed to each other that we would never succumb, even if sorely tempted, because our marriage was too important to both of us.

"I rarely travel so I don't even have much opportunity to cheat, but on one occasion four years ago, it happened. I'm a stockbroker and a number of my clients are in oil, and at the time a large percentage of my own capital was heavily invested in petroleum stocks. I was in Texas wining and dining some clients when I heard that a deal that I was in had gone sour. I would have to sustain tremendous losses. I didn't know where I'd manage to raise the tuition due for my daughter for school the next week. . . . When I went back to my hotel I went to the bar and had several drinks.

"A tall, pretty woman was sitting there and she said to me, 'You look like you've lost your best friend.' We spent the night together."

"Did you tell your wife about it?" I asked. "I would think that under the circumstances, and given your unusual closeness, that she might have understood."

"I couldn't tell her. . . . To say that it haunted me would be an understatement," he replied. "I'd broken a trust.

Even though the sex meant nothing to me, in essence it was like having a human to numb me instead of a drink—anesthetic sex—I couldn't tell Sarah. I think the only reason I can live with the knowledge that I broke a vow is that I know it will never happen again. But I suffer because there's something between us that she will never know."

"I've had a few one-nighters and a couple of 'nooners' over the years," said a man from Denver who has been married for a decade, "and I never thought my wife would know. . . . About six months ago I'd been with someone at our sales conference. We'd been partying and this woman, who was in one of our divisions based in Japan, passed out on the bed in my room. When she woke up, I was still drunk as a skunk but we got it on, in a manner of speaking. My machinery didn't work too well with all that booze. It was nothing, just some harmless physical sex with a woman I would never see again. My wife somehow found out about this. She was really furious, even threatened divorce. She's still plenty angry, but I'm sure we'll iron it out. It's a matter of her understanding it was just sex—nothing more."

Like this man's wife, most women can't conceive of the one-nighter's belief that he is immune to any emotional connection in the sex act. But that's what he professes. He is also convinced that his wife or girlfriend will never find out about his nefarious activities because what's happened usually has happened away from home or in remote, anonymous circumstances. In the unlikely event that she *does* discover what he's been doing, he reasons that she'll be angry and hurt, but not so wrought up that she'll break off the relationship. After all, his thinking goes, he's "basically faithful," a sexual quickie is meaningless.

Thus, for most one-night standers, the guilt or anxiety associated with extramarital sex dissolves or is replaced by a sense of unease that can be disagreeable but tolerable. Some men may have only one or two one-night stands during a long and rich marriage, others may indulge their desires repeatedly. Whatever his pattern, a man almost always characterizes these as "irresistible situations" or very often "the opportunity was there and I couldn't afford not to take it."

The Long-Term Lover

This is a man who, paradoxically, is monogamous with two women. The most drastic example of the long-term lover is the actual bigamist or the man who maintains two families, children, pets, households and all. The more common type of long-term lover is the man who is actually torn between two women, with each of whom he shares an established relationship.

"My wife's name is Andrea, my girlfriend's name is Janice. I sometimes call them Jandrea because she would be the perfect woman for me. I'm faithful to them both, and I can't give up either one," says a man who accurately describes the dilemma of dual monogamy, "I've anguished about this situation for almost seven years. With the energy I've spent having essentially two wives, I could have become president."

A long-term lover does not necessarily view himself as unhappy with his marriage. He may go so far as to say his mate is wonderful, he loves her very much, and he'll often protest that he's quite satisfied with his relationship. But, when prodded, he'll characteristically add *except for*. The "except for" can refer to sex, to intimacy, to fun, to a whole spectrum of needs that he feels his partner cannot fulfill. But in his mind the marriage or relationship is working well enough to sustain him, it's just that he needs more.

"I guess you could call me the type of guy who has extra requirements," coolly allows a man that I interviewed in Los Angeles, "I need a lot of sex and I get it from my girlfriend. I need a stable home life and I love my kids and I get that from my wife. My girlfriend makes noises about me leaving my wife sometimes, but she puts up with me, and I'm sure my wife doesn't suspect anything."

"How is the sex with your wife?" I asked.

"We had an outstanding sexual relationship for three or four years," he said. "I was monogamous, I really didn't need anything or anyone else then. My wife was an incredible lover. She loved doing it. All the time. Anywhere, everywhere. When our first child was born, things cooled off and, of course, that was natural. But I thought it would be temporary. But then we had our second daughter about a year and a half later, and it came down to sex once a week and an obligatory Sunday morning when the kids were at their grandparents. That's when Sheila entered the picture. We had great sex, but it turned into something more, a serious relationship. It's been six years and I can't give her up."

"More" is another one of the long-term lover's operative words. The long-term lover very often describes himself as needing *more* so he can turn to another woman to provide more intimacy, or more or better sex.

Conversely, these men sometimes say that the other woman provides them with an important *less*. Less responsibility, less "static," fewer demands. "She wanted less from me and that's why I love her," says a commodities broker of his long-term girlfriend. "She makes no demands. I always feel my wife expects too much of me. I really believe that the only reason I can maintain my marriage is that Gloria, my girlfriend, is there to ease the responsibilities that I feel are overwhelming me."

There's also a kind of rueful humor involved in the

long-term lover's situation. "As anyone who has had a 'committed affair' will tell you," says a man who sustained a marriage and a mistress as well as a highly demanding job as a magazine publisher, "food is a big problem. I often found myself having two dinners, and the holidays were complete torture. Ironically, I volunteered for a committee to feed the homeless so I could say that I was working on Christmas Day. What I actually did was run to the office to pick up presents I'd left there—thank God the building was open around the clock in case we were working on a late-breaking story—and then I'd run across town to Claudia's and we'd exchange gifts. We'd have champagne and a gourmet dinner, and then I'd come home to the holiday turkey and have to lie about what I'd done for the homeless. I detested myself. Hated myself. I didn't even give money to the homeless, but I kept it up for four years until Claudia gave me a real ultimatum. I couldn't leave my wife, so Claudia left me."

This man, and others who follow the same pattern, lives his days drenched with anxiety, guilt, and hyperstimulation. His emotional life is always high-tension and an immense amount of time and energy is lavished on the intricate and hazardous balancing act between two women and two lives. A long-term lover often uses his wife or children as rationalizations for maintaining the nerve-racking status quo. "She'll go to pieces if I leave her" or "I can't do it to the kids" are two of the long-term lover's most famous phrases.

Therapists often explain the long-term lover's behavior as revolving around "attachment problems." By attaching himself to two women, paradoxically, he is not deeply, intimately connected to anyone. He is keeping both women at a distance. Because so much frantic activity is required to preserve the equilibrium, he cannot see what he is doing. Nor does he want to.

The Occasional Strayer

Between the man who has only one-night stands, which are a form of instant pseudo-intimacy, and the long-term lover who keeps a resolute psychological distance from both his mates, lies the majority of non-monogamous men—those who have short flings or affairs where there is some element of emotional as well as sexual involvement. These are *the occasional strayers.*

The occasional strayer is a man who usually will tell you that he's a "pretty monogamous guy." His is, in fact, a form of qualified or limited monogamy, and he's full of "buts" when questioned more closely about his sexual habits. But for the times he's needed sex, but for the fact he's been on a trip and lonely, but for the night when a knockout woman came on to him and was irresistible and he became involved for several weeks . . . but for these irregularities, he's monogamous.

The occasional strayer might have an "affairette," indulge in an extramarital weekend or a short sexual odyssey. He might begin to wet his toes emotionally, but is convinced he can pull back before the wave of a genuine attachment has formed.

Here's how an occasional strayer describes himself. "Sometimes I need sex, sometimes I need to feel that I am a hot shit, sometimes I need to screw because I'm angry, and those are the times when I do it. I'm always aware that my marriage is most important and that what I'm doing is wrong, but I do it anyway. I'm so concerned about being caught that I make absolutely certain there's no trail. . . . Basically I'm a monogamous guy."

Joel, a thirty-year-old assistant vice president at a Boston bank, has been married three years and twice during that time has had "cursory flings" that he depicts this way. "Once, when my wife was at a regional conference for her company, I met a woman playing golf at the local public course. We shared a beer together and got to talking about my wife being away and her husband being in England. We ended up in bed. I saw her a few more times, but I felt she was falling for me, so I backed off. . . . The other situation was also when my wife was traveling on business. I went back to the same golf course, and goddamn, it happened again with another woman. This time it was only twice."

The one-night stander, the occasional strayer, or the long-term lover usually sticks to his particular style or mode of infidelity. But this does not mean that the long-term lover, for example, might not indulge in an anonymous "quickie" or that the occasional strayer might not end up in a long-term affair.

I've used these three classifications because they're a convenient means of identifying the general characteristics of non-monogamous men. It's fairly obvious that when dealing with a psychological area so steeped in secrecy and guilt, it's always difficult, if not impossible, to tell when a man is being, or has been, unfaithful. You'd have to be a mind reader or a professional with years and years of experience to be able to quickly and accurately perceive the different kinds or styles of infidelity. But it may be helpful to sum up by keeping in mind that each category bears some distinguishing marks.

The one-night stander: This man has casual sexual encounters that involve no emotional attachment or connection. He usually suffers little or no guilt because he perceives his behavior to be covert with almost no chance of discovery. He often rationalizes that he is experiencing a physical release that does no harm to his primary relationship because he's totally uninvolved in what has gone on. He's preoccupied with the chase, he revels in the conquest, and he receives a momentary shoring up or assertion of his masculinity that speedy, anonymous sex provides.

The long-term lover: This man generally feels guilty all the time, but never so contrite that he curtails his outside activities. He can be a particularly attentive husband or lover because he feels ashamed of his connivances and machinations. He will come back from his girlfriend or mistress and make love to his wife—or vice versa—in order to convince himself that both relationships are still on the front burner. He might be a flower sender or present giver, and he often does it in twos, one for his wife, the other for his extramarital mate.

A salesperson at a gift shop on Manhattan's Fifty-seventh Street told me one of her customers found out that her husband had a girlfriend when a jewelry store sent her a silver vase with the wrong card attached to it. "The card was in his handwriting and said, 'For Nora, with love,' and alas, the wife's name was Elaine," she recounted. "She had a lawyer investigate and he found out that the husband was always buying two of everything: one for her, one for the mistress."

The occasional strayer: The outstanding characteristic of this man is that he's a prime target for falling in love with another woman. His is, as I mentioned before, the most common type of extramarital behavior. He plays around—not compulsively and not in the anonymous way of the one-night stander or the committed duality of the long-term lover; he allows himself to become emotionally involved, but he believes he can control the situation as well as his own feelings. He's sadly mistaken on this count and thus the odds are that he's in for trouble. His marriage or primary relationship will inevitably be deeply disrupted by his infidelity. When this happens, however, he and his partner can choose to learn from the experience and begin to build a new and deeper intimacy, as we will see.

When I asked an occasional strayer about his "cursory flings" and what effect he thought they might have on his relationship with his wife, he replied, "To tell you the truth, it's gotten me to thinking. There must be something wrong with my marriage. I made a vow to be faithful and I haven't kept it. I don't know what it is, but something's not right, not the same. I don't know how to answer you at this point in time."

This man put his finger on the problem: Something's not right, not the same. Most men stray because their marriages or relationships, in one or many ways, are not satisfying them. Before we can tackle exactly what that "not-right something" is, we need to know still more about what makes a man non-monogamous.

SEVEN

When, Where, and How He's Most Likely to Be Unfaithful

When He's Most Likely to Be Unfaithful

"I only have eyes for you," says the love song and this delicious monovision exists for most men during the halcyon days of infatuation, that intoxicating time when we're passionately "in love." How long the "monogamy period" lasts and what conditions entice a man to infidelity are the issues to which men address themselves in the following pages.

With few exceptions, a "natural" period of monogamy exists for almost every man when he's first in love. It's the time when he really wants no one else, his entire sexual attention is focused on one woman. He most probably has fleeting thoughts about what it's like to be between silky sheets with the beautiful swingy-haired, big-breasted blonde that he glimpsed out of the corner of his eye, but very rarely—unless he has a problem with sexual addictions—does he act on his fantasies during this time in a relationship.

Having had many discussions with women friends over the years and then talking more specifically with men for my previous books, I had a hunch that this interlude of monogamy lasted about three to four years for most men. I was mistaken.

What I've termed the "natural monogamy period" can be appallingly short. "Four days after I was married," one man told me, "I was on a business trip and it happened. I was in my bed in a hotel room with another woman whom I'd had an affair with a few years before. I had every intention of living up to my wedding vows, but it's just not in my blood, I guess."

"How long were you monogamous?" was one of the questions I posed to men and the following responses are representative of the group that I interviewed. The italics are mine.

"About *two years* after my marriage, I got involved with my sister's best friend. She was looking for a job, and I hired her to work part-time in my office," says a San Diego man.

"About a *year and a half* after we moved in together, I had an off-the-record weekend fling," says a thirty-two-year-old garage mechanic from Washington, D.C. "I'm still living with my girlfriend, but it started a pattern."

The following is how a doctor from a large midwestern city answered my question on the monogamy period. "My girlfriend gave me an ultimatum. Marry me now or kiss off," he explained. "We married even though I wasn't convinced it was right. Friends assured me it was normal to be ambivalent about such a big step and I bought it. I became restless, irritable, and disillusioned *about a year* after my marriage. My wife wasn't very interested in sex and we couldn't talk about it. I rekindled a friendship with a nurse I'd had an affair with before I married. I should have told my wife I was attracted to other women and that we should see a therapist, but even though I'm a physician with some psychological background, at the time it didn't enter my twenty-six-year-old mind."

"*Almost two years* to the day we were married," says a real estate broker. "We had a terrible fight. It was the first serious battle we'd had, something to do with her parents, I can't even remember the details. We didn't speak to each other for days, and the next week I ended up having sex with a client whose house I was trying to sell."

Patrick Fonteyn, a man who claims he has a "very strong sexual drive," remained monogamous for six years, but "*after two years* I became very conscious of other women as potential sex partners. I walked around unhappy and avoided situations where I thought I might be unfaithful because of my conscience. Sex had fallen off, we weren't communicating either physically or verbally, and I finally caved in and had sex with a woman I knew from work."

These are only five quotations from among several hundred, but they have one particular factor in common. *Timing.* Each of these men, and the great majority of the non-monogamous men that I interviewed, agreed on the duration and demise of the "natural" monogamy period. We'll go into detail as to the importance of *why* this occurs in upcoming chapters.

What Makes It Easier for Him to Be Non-Monogamous?

Now that men had told me pretty much when to expect the end of the honeymoon, I wanted to know if there were any specific factors or circumstances that made it easier for a man to slip into infidelity. And indeed there are. Basically, there are two conditions that encourage non-monogamy: life-style and high-risk situations.

Life-style

If his work and/or the kind of life he lives includes a great deal of interface with other people, the probability is obviously high that he will come across someone whom he finds sexually attractive. That simple statement packs more wallop if you keep in mind that it's based on a sound psychological principle called the "mere exposure effect."

The mere exposure effect was documented in 1973 by psychologists S. Saegert, W. Swap, and R. B. Zajonc in an article entitled "Exposure, Context, and Interpersonal Attraction" that appeared in *The Journal of Personality and Social Psychologym*, 25.

The basic idea here is that it's difficult to avoid forming some sort of emotional bond when you come into contact with a person over a period of time. Investigators found that mere exposure to someone else can spark liking and perhaps even loving for that person. Mere exposure doesn't generate physical attraction, researchers concluded, but it does very much enhance emotional unity. And from there, it's not a very big leap to a physical connection.

"If you're out there with other people personally or professionally, it'll almost certainly happen sooner or later," is the way one man cynically estimated the odds of non-monogamy. He was also restating the mere exposure effect. "If women are consistently around you in the workplace, it's virtually impossible not to think about screwing," admits the fifty-year-old managing partner of a distinguished law practice.

The electrician who lives in a small town in Wisconsin, who toils alone or with an assistant during the day, is less likely to find a pool of attractive women than the man who earns his living by selling cosmetics in California. Ditto for the man who is based behind a computer at home or the sole-practitioner architect whose coworkers consist of construction men as compared to an editor at a large publishing house, a television producer, or an associate in an urban law firm.

Here is how one monogamous man who was often exposed to glamorous women finally succumbed. "I'd been married four years and I was totally faithful, even though I'm surrounded by bunches of good-looking, smart, interesting females. I was working on a TV series and one of the extras on the show had been a Miss Universe contestant. Cut to eye contact and smile. We chatted. Her car had broken down and she didn't have a lift back to her apartment. I drove her home and I was terrified because she was open and warm. I thought 'Oh, Jesus, what am I going to do?' but I didn't really think I'd be offered sex. When it became apparent she was interested, I realized I would be committing adultery. I told her I was married and we stopped. She asked me if I was happy. I didn't say anything to her, but I had a problem. My wife wasn't too interested in sex, she was in school and had very little time for the marriage. Here was this beautiful woman offering herself. She was willing, she was available. She wanted me. I wanted to, but I was scared. And then suddenly I decided to go ahead and I did it."

"What happened after that?" I asked after he paused for a few moments.

"I went back and told my wife," he said quietly, "because I wanted to tell her something had happened. It was a way to explain how unhappy I was with our own sex life. She went bananas. I don't think she could hear me even if she had wanted to. . . . Later, after we split up she said to me, 'I should have understood you were trying to make it work for us, but I didn't.' "

In addition to a man's exposure to numbers of women through his job or his profession, his personal life-style can determine whether he has more or less access to the enticements of extramarital sex. "My wife and I do a lot of work in the community," explains a man from Atlanta. "We go to many fund-raisers and benefits, and I meet women who are dying to get laid. They're isolated at home with the kids, and the husband is boring or out-of-town a lot, so they come on to you. If I didn't get around on the social circuit, I'd never know how much is out there just waiting to be had."

Another man who runs a computer business from his apartment rarely sets eyes on women during the day. "But I go bowling," he said, "and I look at women—and they look back. You'd be amazed at how easy it is to get involved with someone who has the same interests as you do. My wife has no interest whatsoever in bowling, doesn't even want to try it, never once came with me to see what the fun was all about. I didn't start bowling to look for sex, but in the end that's what happened."

High-risk Conditions

In addition to the exposure to women in his particular work/play orbit, there are what one man termed "high-risk" conditions that almost certainly can encourage infidelity or, at the very least, churn up the urge for it.

"High-risk" includes circumstances such as these:

"We live in Indianapolis and my wife's parents live about two hours away. Her mother wasn't doing well, and very often she stayed with her parents for a few days to sometimes a week."

"She spends a lot of time playing bridge or shopping with her friends. The woman in the apartment next door would just come over and hang out while Kit was playing cards."

"My coworker just broke up with her boyfriend and she counts on me as her best male friend, so it was natural that I had to see her a lot . . ."

"Skiing is something I really enjoy and my wife hates the cold, so I ended up going to ski resorts without her . . ."

Each of those quotations is from a monogamous man who ended up being unfaithful. "I can't really tell you how it happened," one of them told me. "I believed I would never cheat, and all I can say is that the situation made it impossible to resist." He added this piece of advice, "Tell women that when they're not paying attention to a man, or when they're not *there* for him, it's just too easy for another lady to fill the bill."

Of all the conditions that men describe as "high risk" for infidelity, there is one which is absolutely treacherous: It occurs when he says "I have to stay late at the office."

If I were asked to locate the exact territory at which a large percentage of infidelities take root, it's when he starts working longer hours. This may seem obvious, but when you hear it over and over again as I did in talking with men, you begin to realize just how prevalent the office or work-related affair is—and to what disasters it can lead.

"There are high-risk and low-risk situations," observes a forty-five-year-old monogamous stockbroker from New York. "In business situations you leave early because if you leave late, the atmosphere becomes more charged, more close, more open to connection on an intimate level.

I bring work home if it's a matter of staying late. The few times I left the office after six, I almost broke my life-long pattern of monogamy. If you've made the conscious decision to be faithful, it's easier to withstand pressures, but there are always occasional snares and I think most men who work late in offices can much more easily succumb to them."

"Men delude themselves that they can control not only their own emotions but the other person's as well," says a man who was positive he would never fall in love, even though he had numerous "office flings." "When it happened to me, I couldn't believe it," he recalled. "I realized I loved this woman—who happens to be my assistant—far more than my wife. In fact, trite as it sounds, I felt I had never really been in love before." I heard stories exactly like this one many times over.

The relationships between a man and his secretary, the female "buddy" in the next office, the colleague who works on a deadline project, the coworker who accompanies him on a business trip—these are the "high-risk conditions" that induce a familiarity that is all too easily transmuted into emotional and sexual intimacy.

Keep in mind that the point at which a man is most likely to become unfaithful falls within the eighteen- to twenty-four-month mark. In addition, there are, as we've just seen, several external work and life situations that encourage non-monogamy. Far more formidable and much more mysterious than any of these is the other woman herself. Exactly what is that *powerful something* that lures a man to her?

EIGHT

The Other Woman: What Does He See in Her?

We're all acquainted with the phenomenon: A man has an affair with a woman, perhaps he even leaves his wife and his children and his home for her. Having met a number of these "other women," I've asked myself: *What does he see in her?*

I found myself very often retorting "I don't see much— at least on the surface."

What kept surprising me was how many "other women" are amazingly average-looking or unsexy or not at all charming. One well-disseminated example of this plain-Jane phenomenon was the woman who lured a very powerful and famous man from his beautiful wife and three young children. This "other woman" has been described as having legs "that looked as if they'd been put on upside down"—with a personality to match.

What, exactly, did *she* do, say, or give to this dedicated husband and family man to make him so gaga over her?

This is the question that's endlessly intrigued me and

every one of my friends and it's the same query that I put to men and to experts: What is it that the other woman does or has to make a man fall into bed with her?

Generally, the answers fell into three categories: *magic*, *pure sex*, and *freedom from responsibilities*—and each of these provides a clue to the underlying dynamic of monogamy. However, although men adorn the "other woman" with certain attributes, I came to realize that the attraction is not what he "sees" or finds in her, it's something he *gets* from her.

First, let's explore what men said in answer to my question and then we'll analyze what it actually is that the "other woman" gives to a man to make him nonmonogamous.

She Possesses a "Magical" Attraction

Sharon Stein, a well-known matrimonial lawyer in New York, has been privy to many tales about men's infidelity. "I believe that there are times when a man is unfaithful because someone has a magical, romantic pull for him no matter how happy he is in his marriage. I had a client who had been a completely monogamous man, genuinely content in his relationship, and one day he found himself in my office much to his own surprise and dismay. He wanted an immediate divorce in order to marry another woman."

Did he elaborate on what it was about this woman that made him change his monogamous behavior—and his life—so dramatically, I wanted to know.

"This was an extremely handsome and charmingly modest man," Ms. Stein said. "And it was obvious that women would find him very attractive. And yes, he admitted very often women came on to him, explicitly let him know they were available. This woman, call her Deborah, didn't do anything to entice him, but she was somehow outrageously exciting to him. She simply happened to be there. He wasn't looking and nothing was deficient in the marriage. She was also married and felt the same way too. I believe they were totally helpless. He was powerless in her presence and she was definitely not coming on to him."

Ms. Stein points out this kind of inexplicable enchanted spell, which leads two people through the devastating experience of double divorce, is *extremely rare*. Many men seek dissolution of a marriage claiming they had an "irresistible attraction" to a woman but, in most cases, Stein feels this is a cover-up for considerable uncharted trouble in the intimate territory between husband and wife. "He may claim she bewitched him, but during the separation proceedings, it usually comes out that the marriage was rocky and the other woman was a natural solution to his problems," she says.

A woman who knew of my monogamy project suggested I interview a man who, she believed, had had a similar experience to the one that Stein described about her client. A magical net had fallen over this man during the previous summer and, sadly, with three children under the age of nine, he was in the process of a searingly difficult divorce. Like Stein's client, Jonathan Lee too had been a monogamous man until he met Elizabeth.

I had been forewarned that Jon was a very private person and, given the emotional pandemonium that he was experiencing, I was surprised when he agreed to an interview.

"At age thirty-seven, I believed I had the perfect marriage," he explained, "I was convinced that I had built an incredible life for Cynthia, myself, and my three kids. We were happy living in Los Angeles, and we'd built a beautiful weekend place far off the beaten track where all of us had wonderful times together. We had vacations and good friends. I was stressed but confident about my career. I had an occasional lust but never acted on it. I felt it would be impossible for any other woman to penetrate that life I had so carefully constructed."

"What exactly happened to cause your suddenly wanting a divorce?" I asked.

"Nine months ago I was having a working dinner with a colleague. I wasn't drunk, but I'd had a couple of glasses of wine more than usual. As I was waiting for my car, I came face to face with what I view as the most beautiful woman I've ever seen. Totally out of character, I looked at her and said—out loud—oh, my God. It was as if some spell had come over me. She smiled and we both got into our cars. I followed her and pulled up next to her at a red light. I said something like 'I think I'm drunk, but I want to see you.' She said, 'I think you are, too,' but she agreed to a date to have dinner two nights later.

"I felt that something terrible and wonderful had happened to me. The feelings alternated. I was panicky, a new feeling for me. I called her and asked her if I'd made a fool of myself and she said yes, but we kept the date. And we've never been apart. I told my wife two months after I met Elizabeth that I wanted a divorce."

Could he describe what it was, specifically, about Elizabeth that was so magical? As he talked more about Elizabeth and his soon-to-be ex-wife, I saw a less enchanted marriage than the one Jonathan Lee had first pictured.

As we began to touch on sex I had the feeling that he was becoming uncomfortable. I said something about having interviewed many people about sex and how I'd found that a surprising number of men and women who were married or living together had *very little or no sex over a period of months or even years*. At those words, his face registered a look of surprise and relief.

Yes, he said, he'd had a similar experience. He and his wife had not had sexual relations in three years.

"How did you feel about that?" I asked.

"My marriage appeared on the surface to be very normal," he said, "but there was a great deal of tension underneath. I knew it was strange and unhealthy not to have sex, but I didn't want to think about it, much less admit the problem existed, so I shrugged it off and concentrated on work and the kids and the business perks, which were considerable. My wife is objectively gorgeous, but she's naive about sex. I'm not aggressive sexually, even though people will tell you it couldn't be true because I'm a killer in business. But the real truth is that I would have wanted my wife to come on to me. I couldn't tell her that. She viewed sex as nonrecreational and I saw it as the opposite. In retrospect, I'm finding that for three years I either consciously or unconsciously beat down one of the most important things in life."

"What made it so difficult to ask your wife to come on to you?"

"I don't know. I guess I felt she should know what I needed sexually without my asking for it."

"So Elizabeth really wasn't so inexplicable or magical," I said gently. "Your marriage was in trouble and Elizabeth met a sexual need—"

"You could say that. Yes. She gave me the sex I wanted but even more, she's very assertive in bed, which made a big difference because I'm kind of passive as I said. I want that kind of active sex. She made me feel very, very good about myself."

After my interview with Jon Lee, I spoke with a psychotherapist in Manhattan who had had firsthand experience of being involved with a woman he saw as sexually mesmerizing. "Meeting someone who has a particularly strong sexual impact on you can wreak havoc in your life," he said. "Sometimes it happens that the issue of 'is it going to hurt my spouse' is subordinate to the immense pull you feel in your attraction. You can call it mystical or whatever you like but ninety-nine times out of a hundred this sort of unique cataclysmic sexual attraction raises the issue of problems veiled in the primary relationship.

"This happened to me in my own marriage. I considered myself monogamous and happy with my wife until I met Bettina. She was sexually hypnotic to me. I really felt powerless when I was with her. I knew that this kind of thing usually happens only in novels, so I had to face what was going on in my life and in my own marriage to cause this unexplainable attraction. And I discovered that there were deeper concerns causing trouble between me and my wife. Issues of sex and control and intimacy. We were both willing to work on these and the marriage was saved—and enriched."

All told, I talked with many, many men who declared that what the "other woman" possessed was a magical, compelling quality that drew them inexorably into bed; but when all was said and done, it seemed pretty clear to me that if you look up the other woman's sleeve, you'll observe she's used no trickery—her trump card is simply that she is fulfilling a requisite he has that's not been met in his primary intimate relationship.

"She Gives Me Sex Pure and Simple"

Many men claim that the reason they stray is "pure sex," a "relief from sexual tension," "a way out of sexual boredom." In other words, the answer to my question of "What did you see in her?" is, not surprisingly, sex.

One man's story of infidelity starts out typically, "I

didn't get enough sex with my wife. It was sex pure and simple, that's what Joanne gave me."

Then he went on to describe a particular scene with Joanne: "She told me all the time she just adored sex with me. . . . She knew I loved tea roses. One night we went to the movies and it was a foreign film, and we came to the city and were sitting in the New Yorker theatre. I put my hand inside her pants and I leaned down to kiss her and I smelled tea roses and she had real tea rose petals between her legs. I could fuck her morning, noon, and night."

"Do you consider that 'pure and simple' sex?" I asked.

"Well," he replied, "it's not your everyday bread-and-butter intercourse."

"Could it have been that she knew how to turn you on in a more dramatic way, like hidden tea roses?" I smiled. "Also you said 'She told me all the time she adored having sex with me'—wasn't that a turn-on too?"

"Yes, *she made me feel wanted*. My wife wasn't so interested in *me or sex or maybe the two mean the same thing*." (Italics mine.)

Even when a man strongly asserts that the other woman simply gives him a means of relieving sexual frustration, that it's sex "pure and simple" that he sees in her, it becomes clear, after relatively superficial soul-searching, that there is more to the matter than the purely physical.

The fact that a woman *wants* to sleep with a man, is *willing* to have sex with him, makes herself *available* to him—all of this signals that he is attractive in some way, that he has something to offer, that he possesses a certain power over a woman, that he can be secure, however momentarily, in his masculinity. Even though he may not even know her name or ever see her again, the 'other woman' provides a certain kind of nourishment that he is highly reluctant to pass up.

"She Lightens My Life"

"I always felt there was so much noise at home. Everything was going at once: my wife, the kids, the TV, the telephone. With Roz I could escape. She turned down the volume for me," says a construction worker.

"The thing about affairs is that you don't have to deal with real life," explains another man. "B. wrecked our affair by complaining to me. Once she started griping, it was too much like home. When she acted like a mistress, everything was going fine . . ."

"I couldn't take the pressure," recalls still another man. "I began having little affairs, short flings, to take the burden off myself. The bills piled up, the adjustable percentage on the mortgage adjusted up, and for an hour or two I'd be able to get away from all those problems. . . . My wife likes to get it on, but it seems that we were both too busy with life to have enough time in bed together. So I just started some extracurricular relaxation. Like I said, to get away from the pressure. . . . To answer your question, what Judy gave me was a way out."

What this man is saying is echoed by many others: The "other woman" is a facilitator for dodging real life, she relieves the tedium and anxiety of ennui and most of all, she offers what he sees as freedom and diversion from responsibilities—she eases the load by lowering the pressure and by turning off the noise.

The Secret Gift

Although men impute several fairly obvious lures as part of the "other woman's" kit bag of attractions, her most potent hook is something I eventually came to think of as the "secret gift" she gives to a man. In other words, as I said before, what he "sees" in her is something he *gets* from her.

The story of Arthur Charos helps to give a clearer picture of what this "secret gift" is.

Arthur is a man who had been very non-monogamous during his marriage. "I played around for all the reasons—hot sex, excitement, novelty—but I'm Catholic, I knew I would never leave Shawn," he said.

But he did end his marriage for a woman who "wasn't even as good as Shawn was sexually."

"There was an initial attraction to Sandy," Arthur said, "and we went to bed. No bells went off, but we had a pretty nice time. And I saw her again. Soon it was clear she wasn't just another score. She understood me. She gave me a lot of confidence in myself."

This was an arresting comment from a man who appears to be the epitome of self-confidence. Arthur Charos is a charismatic guy—I happen to think he's one of the sexiest men I interviewed. He has the most wonderful grin, he's great with one-liners, pokes fun at himself, he's in terrific physical shape (an "incredible hunk" say several of his coworkers) and exudes self-assurance. As a partner in a prestigious public relations firm in New York, he lands national accounts with envious ease. His business style—and I've been present at meetings with him—is commanding and authoritative and appealing. It appeared to me that he was a man who really knew his own worth and had a strong ego.

"Just how did she give you confidence?" I asked.

"It was in work," he replied. "I had to give a presentation to a major account and I was nervous—"

"But," I interrupted in honest disbelief, "I've seen you make presentations several times under difficult circumstances and you were incredibly confident. It was contagious, the rest of your staff felt it too."

"That's what you all thought," he said and grinned the disarmingly sexy grin. "But inside I was torn into pieces. I always thought it was going to end up badly. Not only would we not land the account but I'd look like an asshole. I'm a kid from Brooklyn and I've struggled a lot. I get scared sometimes and I get that imposter phenomenon. The night before we were going after a major account, Sandy and I were having dinner together in a romantic restaurant. I told her what was going down at the office and she suddenly said, 'This is a beautiful place, but let's forget eating. We're heading for my apartment to go over what you're going to say.'

"She worked the presentation through with me and she still does it every time I have to do something big. My wife didn't really know what I was involved with at the office. She used to ask and then it stopped. Sandy was aware of everything about my work and she made me feel I could do it. It was obvious: She gave me self-confidence."

Howard Nolton also was attracted to the "secret gift." A tenured professor at an eastern university, Howard described how he became deeply involved with another woman after seven years of sporadic flings.

"My wife is certifiably a brilliant person and she's very articulate, but she wasn't verbal about how attractive I was. I didn't get any feedback from her. I always felt a little shortchanged when they handed out good looks. She didn't make comments about me physically and she also never said anything about sex. . . . I found this second woman instantly attractive. And I think it was because one of the first things she said to me was what great eyes I had. It may sound superficial and unimportant, but I felt like a tree in a forest and I fell over immediately. I wanted a reaction to *me*, I needed the kind of response that my wife never gave me."

So, exactly what is it that the other woman does to

make a man fall into bed with her? Some men say sorcery, others say sex, others proclaim she's a flight from the real world.

Divorce lawyer Sharon Stein is the person who ultimately gave the best answer.

"The other woman is generally ego-boosting and reassuring," says Stein. "She's figured out that the male ego has to be stroked and she strokes. She makes a man feel important, sexy, worthwhile. . . . You might even think of her as a variation of Marilyn Monroe. Monroe emphasized the sex aspect to make a man feel self-confident. There are many other ways to do it, but that's usually the one means to make him feel important and special immediately."

Wives whose husbands leave them, Stein underscores, often take their husbands for granted. "Women's lives are so complicated and full of anxiety and stress. But men are under so much pressure too nowadays," she says. "It's so exhausting to struggle up the ladder or be on the top rung that there's a terrible need to have someone tell you 'You'll make it!' and to give you the feeling that you deserve to be there.

"Men," sums up Ms. Stein, "seek other women to feel good about themselves."

"Isn't that really another way of describing the secret gift I mentioned to you earlier?" I asked her. "The secret gift is what makes a man fall into bed with another woman, the secret gift is—"

"What he gets from the other woman is self-confidence and self-esteem," Stein finished my sentence, "and women have forgotten how important these are. What a man sees—and seeks—in the other woman is a strengthening of his sense of himself, his worthwhileness."

NINE

The Boy, the Adolescent, the Man

Throughout the preceding pages you've read the words of men I've talked with over the past two years. What's to be concluded from all these interviews? First of all, you've learned about why men are *not* monogamous. Men told me they were unfaithful because their marriages or relationships were strained, because sex was bad at home, that tensions and responsibilities of everyday life could be alleviated by brief encounters or long-term affairs. You've also read about men who affirm their need for continuing shots of self-confidence and men who say that their mates take them for granted, and that the "other woman" is an ego-builder.

Experts in the field of intimacy and relationships underscored what the men I interviewed told me. Many studies have been done on infidelity. Two in particular discuss the most frequently given motivations for extramarital sex. Anthony Thompson, in an article entitled "Extramarital Sexual Crisis: Common Themes and Therapy Implications" (*The Journal of Marriage Therapy*, Winter, 1984), and also Bernard L. Greene, Ronald R. Lee, Noel Lustig in "Conscious and Unconscious Factors in Marital Infidelity" (*Medical Aspects of Human Sexuality*, September 1974),

discuss the most frequently given motivations for
extramarital sex. These are
    curiosity
            need for variety
                sexual frustration
                    boredom
                            need for acceptance and
                                recognition.

In addition to the formal studies on infidelity, the experts that I personally interviewed were also in general
agreement about what made men stray. "Boredom with
the quality of sex in the relationship and the promise
of having something enjoyable that's not available at
home," is the way a marriage counselor phrased the
grounds for non-monogamy that he hears most often in
his practice. Another therapist simply concluded, "If
he has an affair, he's trying to extricate himself from the
responsibilities of the marriage because something is
wrong with that relationship."

When you turn to the monogamous man and begin
to dissect the information gathered from those interviews,
a different kind of blueprint begins to emerge. *My wife/
girlfriend understands me, the sex continues to satisfy me, she
interests me as a person, she makes me feel good, she bolsters
my ego*—these refrains replay throughout the interviews
of men who are faithful.

Now that you're more familiar with the deeper reaches
of both monogamous and non-monogamous males, it's
time to explore the basic ego needs of both men and
women. These ego needs shape the psychosexual dynamics
that occur in every intimate male/female relationship.

As I mentioned at the beginning of this book, the anatomy of the male ego is critically different from that of
the female's—men have certain ego needs and women
have others. Once the basic differences are clear, you'll

be able to understand a surprisingly simple principle—
that of fulfilling ego needs—both his and yours. And it
is this feeding and nurturing of "the hungry ego" that,
as we'll see, forms the basis for a rich and meaningful
monogamous relationship.

Dr. John Baer Train is the man who first articulated the
notion of "the hungry ego." He looks a lot like a ge-
nial Sigmund Freud without the goatee. In fact, Freud's
picture hangs over his desk. Across the room, over the
chair where patients sit (no couch was in evidence), in
the doctor's direct line of sight is a portrait of Moses.
Past president of the American Society of Psychoanalytic
Physicians, a well-known psychiatrist and distinguished
analyst with forty years of practice, Dr. Train is a tall,
imposing silver-haired man with the gentlest manner.

At our first interview, as I introduced myself, he
warmly shook my hand and bade me to make myself
comfortable in an easy chair next to his desk.

"So you think a man can be monogamous?" he asked
with a smile.

"Do you?" I responded.

"Yes," he replied. "If you know the psychosexual dynamics that go on between a man and a woman."

"I'd need several more years in graduate school for
that," I laughed.

"No, it's a basically very simple idea," he said, "but
let me say something before I explain. A little 'lecturette'
if I may, okay with you?"

"Sure," I said.

"Marriage is an institution," he began, "although we
would not choose to live in institutions. Marriage gives
us an enlargement of ourselves through the connection
with the other person. We seek in marriage all of what
we've wanted since childhood, through adolescence and
into adulthood. If we understand this idea, a person
will know what he or she needs and what their partner

is looking for as well. Both partners gain from marriage, but in order to have a marriage that is solid and well structured, it requires monogamy."

"And how is monogamy possible?" I asked.

"Every spouse must take into consideration the needs of their mate to the same degree that they would take their own needs into consideration."

"The golden rule?" I said.

"Yes, psychosexually," he nodded, continuing. "In order to fulfill these basic needs, a woman must acknowledge that part of the institution of marriage is the nurturing of her husband's ego.

"A woman must recognize that her mate is part boy, part adolescent, part man. The boy in him wants to know that she really cares for him and his well-being. The adolescent wants to know that he's the object of her whole sexuality; the mature man wants to know that she's proud of him, approves of him. In essence it's a continuous nurturing through life. What keeps us together is nourishing of each other's ego needs. You could make long lists of what these things are in everyday life, but it's not really necessary. As long as you understand the fundamental dynamic, you simply need to use common sense in fulfilling those needs.

"When two people love each other, they have dropped their ego guards and they are vulnerable to hurt each other. We can now understand why, if two people never argue or fight, they can't love each other because they have not dropped their guards. But an argument or fight should never become so drastic or destructive as to undermine the ego of another. Once the ego is undermined, it's easy to meet another woman and say 'my wife doesn't understand me' and non-monogamy follows."

"You mean it all comes down to feeding his ego?" I asked.

"A man must understand that a woman needs her ego

supported and nourished," Dr. Train replied. "She deserves exactly the same thing as she gives."

"But she's the one who must do the giving—first," I said.

"Let me answer that this way," he continued. "It's been said that for a man, a primitive sense of masculinity is fulfilled through sexuality whereas the primary establishment of femininity for a woman lies in her being loved. Whether we agree with this or not, any survey indicates this is so. If a woman wants to be loved, wants monogamy, yes, she is usually the one who begins—and maintains—the nourishing process."

"Please let me stop you for a moment," I said, "I want to get this clear. If you understand the psychosexual dynamic between a man and a woman, you'll be able to diminish the chances of infidelity, right?"

"Right," he said, smiling.

"And that psychosexual dynamic is based on this simple idea. The ego is needy. It has to be cared for. When the ego is hungry, not being fed, the chances are that a man will be unfaithful, right?"

"Exactly," he said. "To put it in the positive sense, if the ego is nourished and attended to, the odds of monogamy are very high."

Dr. Train's clarification of the theory of the hungry ego squared with all my research. It was the substructural premise of what every man had divulged in countless interviews. "The way to a man's heart is through his stomach" turned out to be a shrewd psychosexual metaphor.

As Dr. Train finished, I remembered two particular interviews with monogamous men.

The first was with a business executive who explained to me why he was monogamous. "My wife adores me, she does everything for me and I adore her for it," he had said. "Fifteen years ago I was thin and cute. She flipped over me. She still finds me attractive. It starts with sex and goes on from there if the woman knows what to do. And my wife does know what to do. She has the gift of the courtesan. She's never threatening or intimidating. She is constantly nourishing the sense of who I am. Women have been a civilizing force for two thousand years, and suddenly that wonderful womanly thing that women have always done and men have adored has become a bad thing. That wonderful thing is taking care of one's husband. That's what my wife does and that's why I have been monogamous—totally monogamous—for twenty years."

The second interview was with a monogamous man from San Antonio, Texas. Jackson Avery's words could sound insufferably macho and chauvinistic—unless you understand the concept of nurturing the hungry ego.

"My wife lets me be who I am by keeping herself out of the conversation," was how he lead off our talk. "My wife doesn't vie for dominance of role. The role is never in question. The woman lets the man be dominant, she doesn't imply that she's smarter or wiser. Keeping the 'I' out of the conversation keeps the competitiveness and worry away. It's one less person I have to compete with. The man has his balls on the line all the time. He's competitive, it's scary. Bring back my sensitivity, my sense of self, encourage me. It starts with sex, but you have to keep letting your husband know you're crazy about him."

Now you can hear both these men's words in a different way. And now you can see that their wives were no emotional doormats. In fact, both were high-powered businesswomen with young children—and, very importantly, each had recognized that their mates were "part boy, part adolescent, part man." They knew that, as Dr. Train had said, "The boy in him wants to know that she really cares for him and his well-being. The adolescent wants to know that he's the object of her whole sexuality; the mature man wants to know that she's proud of him, approves of him. In essence it's a continuous nurturing through life."

Both Jackson Avery, the tall Texan, and the other man I quoted happened to be physically attractive as well as successful in their careers. Women would find them extremely appealing both sexually and professionally—as I did. Actually, the two men admitted to being the object of women's attention, but their wives had instinctively understood the psychosexual dynamic—nourish the hungry ego—and their husbands had remained staunchly monogamous.

I recalled the two interviews for Dr. Train. "There you have some good examples of what I was talking about," he nodded, smiling. "It's all in the psychosexual dynamic of meeting ego needs."

I left Dr. Train's office and was rehashing all this information as I walked back to my own. One point the doctor had raised gave me pause. His statement "If a woman wants to be loved, wants monogamy, yes, she is the one who usually begins—and maintains—the nourishing process" bothered me. Women, I thought, as I sat down to transcribe the notes from the interview, end up doing most of the work.

What you will soon realize—as I did from Dr. Train's ideas on the hungry ego—is that the reason we bear the responsibility for relationships, and the reason we require monogamy, has to do with our own female ego needs. In the next chapter we'll learn precisely what the ego needs of both sexes are.

TEN

Our Secret Selves

What is an ego? The way I'm using the word it means *your sense of self, who you are, your identity.* That ego, as Dr. Train explained, must be carefully attended to. "Everybody's got a hungry heart" is the way Springsteen belts it out, and he's psychosexually right on target.

Egos have a structure; they have forces—or needs—that form them. I'm convinced that the male ego has a different structure than the female one. Common sense, simple observation, and hundreds of interviews tell me this and contemporary representatives of Darwinian thought and psychotherapeutic theory also confirm it.

I believe the male ego is built on certain core needs:

Sex

Power

Achievement

Conquest

In order to feel good about himself as a man, to enhance his sense of self-worth and self-esteem, these ego foundations must be buttressed, nourished. Let's start with a brief exploration of sex, power, achievement, and conquest in terms of today's man.

As a boy, a male is brought up with competitive, aggressive practices. He plays games, he's on teams, it's important to win.

A young man's first sexual encounter is a conquest, another form of a game. His first "win" is a girl—if he has to use "love" in order to score, he will. As a man, he will experience sex in terms of ego glow, achievement, beating the competition. *A man's masculinity is confirmed through sex.*

The story is very different for females. A girl or young woman's first sexual experience is not the initial entry on a tally sheet; it's a discovery that opens up a whole new world to her—she sees the potential of caring and intimacy. Her identity, her *sense of femaleness is rooted in love and loving.* Although young girls today are encouraged to become more competitive, you just have to watch a child with her doll to see that nurturing—and society's encouragement of it—is still a critically important part of a female's childhood experience. Thus it seems clear to me that

Love

Loving

Being loved

are the central foundations, the core ego needs for a woman. Again, I base these ego needs on common sense, my own personal experience, and the affirmation of psychologists, psychoanalysts, and anthropologists.

Dr. Ethel Spector Person, a psychiatrist practicing in New York, author of *Dreams of Love and Fateful Encounters: The Power of Romantic Passion,* in a recent essay entitled "Love Triangles" (*The Atlantic Monthly,* February 1988), asserts essentially the same primary idea. "For women, the passionate quest has usually been interpersonal, and has generally involved romantic love; for men it has more often been heroic, the pursuit of achievement or power." Further, she adds, there is a "crucial distinction between the female search for feminine identity through intimacy and the male search for masculine identity through achievement."

Here's the same notion in different words: "The male is commonly of the opinion that the prize is sexual engagement," writes Dr. F. Gonzalez-Crussi in *On the Nature of Things Erotic* (Harcourt Brace Jovanovich, 1988). "To win is to bed. Once copulation has been achieved the game is over. He has 'scored.' The female is not so coarse. Women have yet to divest themselves of the deeply ingrained conviction that the end of seduction is to inspire love."

Some experts propose that the ancient Oedipal conflicts are the causes of this profound difference between the sexes; others conclude that reproductive roles and survival of the fittest are the reasons; still others have a big problem with, and even deny, the existence of any disparities. Arguments can, and will, rage on: They're intellectually engaging, but ultimately, I believe they're beside the point. You may agree with the idea of the different structures of male and female egos or you may hate the very concept— but, again, I believe if you want monogamy, you can take this information and make effective use of it.

What we need to keep in mind is that monogamy is integrally connected to a woman's ego needs for intimacy, love, and loving. A man's ego needs, as I've said, are different: His identity is directly bound up in his sexuality and his sense of achievement. Sex is pivotal to maleness or, to say it still another way, sex to a man means being a man—that's why sex is so all-important to him. "Fucking makes me a man" is the succinct terminology used by a Brooklyn construction worker.

Okay, so now we have two different ego structures with two differing sets of needs. If your ego is hungry for loving and being loved and his is hungry for conquest, achievement, power, sexuality, how do you reconcile those appetites?

You'll be giving love and getting love if you grant your man what his ego requires. You're not sacrificing yourself to fulfill his needs—you're satisfying your own ego cravings to love and to nurture by satisfying his.

When the ego is hungry, when it's not being fed, its owner is very likely to be discontented—and not monogamous. If a woman wants an intimate, loving, faithful relationship, I believe she must realize this is a basic psychosexual imperative she has. To put it into other words: To ultimately gratify *our* own core needs, we must satisfy our lover's psychosexual needs. "A woman," Dr. Train had said, "must acknowledge that part of the institution of marriage is the nurturing of her husband's ego."

Thus the basic "strategy" that I've alluded to in the preceding pages is:

Feed His Ego

Wait just a minute here, you might say. Isn't this a humiliating throwback to the days when Marabel Morgan's book *The Total Woman* (Fleming H. Revell, Co., 1973) counseled females to be sexy and greet their husbands at the door swathed in nothing but see-through Saran Wrap? Isn't this just another way of catering to the "fragile male ego"? Isn't this another load that we have to carry—and the men are all but excused from duty?

Absolutely not.

In no way do I feel that we should retreat to so-called traditional values where roles are stereotyped and the institution of marriage is narrowly defined. But I believe if we want monogamy and intimacy, we, not men, bear the responsibility to attain them. Until there are some basic changes in our society—or in the structure of egos—it seems clear to me that we are the custodians of close relationships.

But isn't feeding his ego very manipulative? Before that can be answered, consult *Webster's* on "manipulate." You'll find it's defined as a) to manage or utilize skillfully and b) to control or play upon by artful, unfair, or insidious means, especially to one's advantage.

Yes, in feeding his ego, you are managing skillfully and doing something for your own purposes. But is it to a man's disadvantage? Isn't it to your advantage—and his— to feed his ego?

The reality of today's relationships is that we *do* shoulder the larger burden for everything—from planning social engagements and initiating long-overdue discussions to making time for sex. We all desperately want our men to pull their weight in managing a marriage but intelligent, pragmatic, monogamously mated women who tell me that their marriages are genuinely happy and satisfying also admit they're the ones who bear the primary— not the total—responsibility as relationship guardians and, although they don't usually admit it, they are consciously or unconsciously using the "feed the ego" strategy.

As women, we have options that were unavailable to us a decade ago. Today our roles in society are not preordained; we have fought to be able to make choices; but I believe that if we don't choose the "role" of protector of intimacy, we are, in essence, slamming the door on the possibility of improvement in relationships between men and women—and the probability of fulfilling our basic needs for love and intimacy and monogamy.

Up to now, culture and tradition dictated that we "satisfy" men. Today, through our knowledge of psychology, it becomes clear that in satisfying a man—in feeding his ego—we will be also deeply satisfying ourselves. Feeding, nurturing, and loving are components of the human female's primal need to love and be loved. To say it one last time: In nurturing and feeding a man's ego, our own ego needs for love and being loved are being met. We don't have to twist ourselves in Saran Wrap to please a man; today's woman has the option to wear whatever she wants. It's not your duty to feed a man's ego, it's your choice.

If you're aware of how and why your mate is turned on by Saran Wrap, for example, you can elect to drape yourself in it—or throw the roll out the window if that's what you want to do. We are aware, sophisticated, and knowledgeable: It is up to each of us to decide for ourselves whether we want to "feed his ego" in order to secure an intimate, monogamous relationship for ourselves.

One very important point must be reemphasized here: Women are not the cause of infidelity nor should we be victimized by it. It doesn't happen because we're not sexy or savvy enough. It happens because a man's basic ego needs are not being met. *But certain men are—or will be—unfaithful because of unmet needs that no woman can meet.* These men are "The Unreachables," the womanizers, the sexual addicts, the deeply neurotic men who require extensive psychological repair work. The ego needs of these men are out of whack. They need too much—or too little. Only a competent therapist can help to return their ego needs to a healthy equilibrium.

Too many authors and authorities today point the finger at women as in some way "deficient" and men, on the other hand, as oafish and "unaware," furthering the mistrust of ourselves and our relations with men. Infidelity is an ugly, painful—and real—possibility in a relationship, but today we are able to choose to do something to help prevent it.

Exactly *how* do you go about applying the strategy of feed-the-ego to get your man to be monogamous? How can you make feed-the-ego work in your own day-to-day life? Before we turn to the answers, let's take a look at some case histories where ego needs were disregarded and examine the consequences of that malnourishment.

ELEVEN

Hungry Hearts

As I talked to therapists, psychologists, and marital counselors about monogamy and ego needs, I amassed scores of stories that exemplified the basic dynamic of feeding—or starving—the ego. Three from my files fill the following pages. The first is about Donna and Stephen Wicker who had a seemingly insoluble problem.

Steve Wicker is a marketing director of a Cincinnati-based retail chain. A graduate of the University of Ohio, where he fell in love with Donna when they were both seniors, a national wrestling finalist, and an avid gardener, he's been married for nine years. During that time Steve and his wife have had one very major problem: Steve would like Donna to wear sexy underwear. *Very* sexy underwear.

"What he wants makes me feel whorish," she told the counselor whose help they finally sought because the marriage was in stormy straits. "I'm not against great-looking lingerie, but the kind he's talking about has holes for the nipples and slits in the crotch. He's also hung up on black garter belts and stockings—and I hate this stuff."

Steve was turned on by the classic trappings of the courtesan and felt that Donna was a rigid prude. "She's uptight and wouldn't even try any of it on," he said. "I tried to tell her it was in the spirit of fun, that we'd both have great times with her wearing that kind of lingerie, but her reaction was always stony. I stopped talking about it, but I kept on fantasizing."

"Donna and Steve had reached an impasse. He was looking at women in his office and imagining them stripping off scanty bras and bikinis while his wife wrapped herself in flannel nightgowns and took to sleeping in the guest bedroom. She felt he wanted to degrade her; he believed she was an ice goddess. Even though he very much wanted to live up to his commitment to monogamy, he was one hop away from an affair that probably would have blown the whole marriage apart," said the therapist I interviewed who had worked with the couple.

"What happened?" I asked. "Can you get someone to change their attitude about such a loaded issue? Or do both have to do it?"

"In this case," she answered, "it was a matter of recalibrating both Steve's and Donna's attitudes about sexuality and sexual fantasy in particular. We started by exploring what sexual fantasy meant to Donna. She said she never had fantasies; she loved Steve, and that was enough to turn her on. Steve, for his part, had an active fantasy life. Plus he was drawn to erotica that ranged from *Penthouse* and *Playboy* to books of drawings by Egon Schiele, the Viennese artist who depicted very sexual women who, as a matter of fact, often wear black stockings and nothing else."

"Did Donna really have no fantasies?" I asked.

"She thought sexual fantasies were, by definition, kinky, so she felt she had never fantasized. She didn't have images of whips and chains or hot underwear or lesbian play, but she actually did have a typically female sexual fantasy, which had to do with a romantic lover, and Steve, when they courted, and in the first few years of marriage luckily filled that fantasy perfectly."

"Well, how exactly did they reconcile their vastly differing viewpoints?" I asked.

Once again, it came down to the needy ego. Steve wanted to feel he was a highly sexual man, a lover for whom a woman would do anything to please, including wear "whorish" underwear. Steve needed to fulfill his fantasies in order to feel more masculine.

"Those fantasies were not harmful or dangerous as, say, rough sex might be," the therapist pointed out, "so what we worked on was getting Donna to be empathetic to her husband's needs."

"But what about her needs?" I asked.

"Her need was to have a romantic lover. And Steve was that very often. Just as she can expect him to be a romantic lover, he can expect her to be a whore in bed."

"How did it work out?"

"It took time to desensitize her to his fantasies so that she wouldn't feel, as she put it, 'defiled' by him. The first step was the underwear itself. We discovered that if she bought it, she was happier about wearing it. She felt she was more in control of what she was doing. That she was the one who was equally calling the shots by, for example, coming home with pink and red lace instead of black. I wish I could report that she loves sporting that kind of underwear, but she doesn't—yet. What she does love is that Steve is paying full-time attention to her sexually and the marriage is back in balance."

"Could she ever feel comfortable in that kind of underwear?" I wanted to know.

"Yes, it's very possible," the therapist replied. "She already sees the difference the acceptance of it has made in the relationship, and in time, I think she'll feel a greater pleasure in being part of Steve's sexual fantasies, and the underwear will just become one element of the sexual play between them."

If Donna Wicker was highly resistant to the trappings of the world's oldest profession, her male counterpart might be Mason Taylor. Until his recent separation, Mason lived in Alexandria, Virginia, with his wife Victoria who is a very un-Victorian woman.

Mason, brought up in a strictly religious household, is an extremely modest man. He avoids being seen nude, although he has a perfectly presentable physique. His wife Victoria is his opposite in this respect. Athletic and sports oriented from early childhood, she's comfortable with her body and often runs around the house with no clothes on. Her intention is not in any way erotic, it's just been a habit of hers since grammar school days. He has told her he dislikes her nudity and she playfully teases him about being so prudish. He doesn't enjoy being teased about this and has said so to Victoria, but she continues her razzing and nude ways thinking Mason couldn't be so serious about something as harmless as walking naked through her own home.

Mason, a government employee, found a woman in his office extremely attractive. He was charmed by her Laura Ashley dresses, her crossed knees, her modest ways. He considered it a great challenge to make her warm and affectionate, and he proceeded to try and seduce her. She resisted for a while, but eventually they began an affair.

When Mason asked for a divorce several months later in order to marry the other woman, his wife, Victoria, was aghast and devastated. She believed her husband was totally monogamous. "Mason's a deeply religious man," she said, "and monogamy was one of his values. The sex in our relationship was a little restrained for me, but basically I thought it was pretty good, and I had absolutely no idea that he was even seeing another woman.

He told me that she was very, very sexual. I couldn't believe it; I've seen her and she's bony and too thin, a prim and proper librarian type."

Was there anything Victoria could have done to avoid the impending divorce? I asked the Washington therapist who did crisis counseling for Victoria after Mason had left her.

"If she had conceded to his moral values, probably the marriage could have been kept intact," she said. "Her own values were not being compromised by what he wanted—a little more modesty— so it would not have been difficult for her, but she just didn't perceive how important his needs in that area were."

"But just how important is his need to have her covered up? It seems a minor point to me too," I said.

"His ego structure was involved with her nudity. He couldn't take it. What was happening was that in walking around nude, she was actually de-eroticizing herself for him. It was destroying his sexual desires. He needed to be able to seduce a woman by slowly taking off her clothes, unmasking the sexual being who hides beneath the prim exterior. Some men might be turned on by the sight of their wives walking around nude. And Victoria's body was in very good shape indeed—but this man needed a high degree of modesty from a woman to really arouse him. The other woman's figure was objectively not nearly as attractive as his wife's, but she fulfilled the basic need he had for demureness in order to make him feel more sexual and more masculine."

"I understand about his needs, but I just must ask about hers," I pursued. "She felt the need to be free of clothing, to walk around nude—"

"But it wasn't an ego issue with her. For him it was really a sexual matter, for her it was just a habit."

"Right," I said, recognizing the validity of her point.

It was less important to her to be naked than for him to have her covered up.

"One more question," I said. "She described him as being restrained sexually, so she must have been somewhat frustrated herself; in other words, *her* needs were not being met. Could she have ever satisfied him and herself?"

"Yes, she could have slowly eroticized him to meet her own needs. If she had covered up her body—which, don't forget, he had actually told her he wanted her to do—he would then have responded in a more sexual way to her because he would have found her more arousing. As she became more desirable to him, their sexual experiences would have been heightened and she could then have made her needs known in this more receptive atmosphere. She found him restrained because he was restrained—turned off would be more accurate—by her nudity."

"So, in meeting his needs, she would have ended up feeding her own ego sexually too."

"Correct," she said. "The significant thing to remember in this case is that his needs were not in conflict with hers. She wasn't morally opposed to walking around with clothes on, it was just her style. But to him it was a much more basic issue, as I said before. She wouldn't have felt personally or morally compromised by what he wanted. She wasn't listening. She just didn't pick up on all the cues he was giving her, up to and including the obvious one of his saying he'd much rather she wore clothes more of the time."

"Even though she didn't have the concept of ego-feeding to go by, if she'd just listened to him and acted on what she heard, the demure one in the Laura Ashleys wouldn't have had much of a chance and they'd still be together. A lot of people would have been saved a lot of suffering," I remarked.

"Yes, that's true. Victoria never wanted the marriage to end, but it was too late; he'd fallen in love with the other woman," she replied.

Many other histories about unmet needs and the temptations—and consequences—of infidelity abound in my notebooks and on my interview tapes. If only I'd known earlier about the concept of the hungry ego, I could have used that knowledge in my own case—to save myself and Chris from a great deal of suffering.

I was deeply in love with Chris and had been living with him for a little less than a year. In order for us to be together, he had made the move to New York from the West Coast and he missed Los Angeles badly. It was his first winter here in the East, a frigid February, the temperatures lingered in the single digits, the gray sky seemed especially sullen, and "windchill factor" was a phrase he had learned to loathe. He had to return to California for a week or so to finish up a project he'd been working on. I couldn't travel with him because I was on a heavy deadline and there was no way I could change my schedule.

This was the first time since we'd been together that I was under exceptional pressure to finish a particularly intractable article. I had been preoccupied with it before he left, and I had to admit to myself that I was relieved at being alone to work without interruption. It was also the first time we'd been away from each other and I missed him tremendously. We talked two, sometimes three, times a day during the week he was gone. He loved LA, he said, but even with slush and snow and the inhumanity of the subway, he was glad that he lived with me in New York.

We celebrated his return with champagne and a trip uptown to hear Bobby Short at the Cafe Carlyle. Two nights later we had friends coming for dinner, and the editor who was working on my story phoned with some revisions she felt were necessary. I started going over the material with her with one eye on the clock, as our guests were arriving in ten minutes and dinner was a long way from being cooked. As we talked an operator broke in on the line.

"I have an emergency call for Chris Franklin," she said tersely.

"Who is it please?" I asked, my heart pounding. I'd never had an emergency interrupt before.

"Gina Walker," a woman's voice could be heard behind the operator's.

My editor said she'd call back later and I ran to the kitchen to put Chris on the phone.

"Yes," he said when he picked up the receiver, "No . . . it's not possible. I thought I explained it as thoroughly as I could . . ." His tone was businesslike but strained.

At that second I knew with certainty he'd slept with Gina Walker and that she was pleading with him on the phone to come back to Los Angeles.

"No," he said again in a patient but firm tone. "It's something that can't be done. We've got guests due in five minutes, so I'm going to hang up—" Another pause while she must have tried to keep him on the phone. He was listening intently. "I'm sorry, I have to say goodbye," he said with finality. And he replaced the receiver on its hook.

I had never met Gina Walker, but Chris had told me about her. She was an exceptionally bright lawyer and he'd worked with her on several deals. He'd also mentioned he'd had a business dinner with her in Los Angeles last week.

"What was that all about?" I asked as coolly as I could. The palms of my hands were gummy with anxiety.

"She wants to push through a project that will never work—" "And," I interrupted, failing to keep the edge out of my voice, "she needs to do it via an *emergency* call?"

The doorbell rang before he could answer. Our guests had arrived.

Fury, fear, dread, resentment snaked through my stomach during dinner. I couldn't eat. I couldn't look at Chris. If our friends hadn't been there, I don't know what I would have done.

I had no proof of what I felt to be true. Chris had told me she had called about a project. Chris was in love with me, I was sure of that. I also was sure—until two hours ago—that we had a monogamous relationship. How could I talk to him about this? How could I avoid being a shrew and screaming and ranting when that's exactly what I felt like doing? I violently hated Gina Walker. The feeling was so physically intense that I couldn't get warm. My body temperature had dropped and my hands actually shook slightly. My feet were damp and cold. The idea that she'd placed an *emergency* call to our home so enraged me that I could hardly control myself.

When we closed the door on Paula and Steve, I said as evenly as I could, "Please tell me the truth. Please. Did you sleep with Gina when you were in Los Angeles? I need to know. Please."

Every kind of emotion assaulted me as I waited for his answer. I wanted to hit him. I wanted to kiss him. I wanted to do violence to her. I couldn't stop obsessing about the *emergency* call. I wanted to cry. I wanted to hiss. I wanted it all to go away. I waited for his response.

"No, it was just business, I told you," he said. "I'm going to do the dishes."

He was lying.

I turned my back on him and went straight to the bathroom. I was so physically tense that I ran a hot bath to

relax and to warm up and tried to think of what to do
or say next.

A few minutes later, he came into the bathroom and
sat on the edge of the tub.

"Yes, I did sleep with her. I don't know how to explain it. It was just sex. She doesn't mean anything. I
love you."

In the days that followed, I attacked. Then I with-
drew. Then I gave him the silent treatment. Finally, we
talked. If it was just sex, I kept wanting to know, then
why did she call you—she knew we were living together, didn't she? She must have based her call on some
deeper emotional connection you had with her. She tel-
ephoned, he said, because she must have thought there
was more to it. But there wasn't. It was just sex.

Even if *you* were clear it was just sex, I reasoned, with
cold hatred of both of them, it was obvious that *she*
didn't. Therefore, it must have been more than *just sex*.
If it was just sex, couldn't you wait a week, just one
week, to have sex with me. And over and over it I went.
With him and with myself.

Finally my anger subsided enough for me to listen to
what he had to say about Gina. Chris had had a brief
affair with Gina years before I'd met him. Then they'd
worked together as good pals. When he went back to
Los Angeles, he'd run into her and they decided to have
an early supper together so he could get her legal take
on the project he was working on. She suggested cooking at her place so they could review the contracts, and
they ended up in bed. Sex had been terrific with her years
before, he said, and it felt satisfying to have a "good
workout" and that's all it was.

But there *was* more. Although Chris was genuinely in
love and committed to me, he very slowly admitted he
thought I was "somewhat naive" sexually.

This threw me. I believed I was a fairly sophisticated

woman and that I was a true giver in bed. He said yes, of course I was, but I could learn more . . .

I did learn more, thanks to the fallout from the Gina Walker affair, plus a great deal of research. Those investigations and labors on behalf of love and sex were incorporated into my first book, *How to Make Love to a Man*, but it was not until I began the interviews for this book—and after I'd begun to understand the principle of the hungry ego—that I realized what other reasons had come into play that caused Chris to end up in Gina Walker's arms in Los Angeles years ago.

Chris had felt alienated from me for the first time since we'd known each other, as I was concentrating on my work more than I was on him. He was feeling adrift emotionally and neglected sexually. He was having a tough time with work adjustments and felt confined in a small apartment in a new and difficult city. I was aware of the problems he had in leaving his home and I was completely sympathetic to them, but I did not know that he felt sexually shortchanged, and that he was so deeply worried about finances, and that his self-confidence— which I'd been so attracted to when I met him—had been eroded by a series of subtle professional setbacks. I believed that, since we talked for hours, we had an uncommon amount of intimacy, and I thought I knew quite clearly how he felt about almost everything. Although we'd never discussed monogamy, I assumed, since we were living together and would eventually marry, that he felt as strongly about it as I did.

It had been a year since we'd been under one roof, two years since we'd been introduced, and we were at a critical juncture where infatuation was giving way to a real intimacy, although at the time I wasn't aware of the stages of love relationships. I had recently begun to notice signs that Chris felt unsettled; he'd sent me a few verbal distress bulletins, but I had decided to attend to those problems as soon as my article was completed. I was engrossed with work, worried about money myself, and not so pleased with finding—figuratively speaking—a pile of Chris's unexpected wet towels on my bathroom floor.

Now that I look back on it, even though I dismissed many of the pressures on Chris as normal adjuncts of New York living, inside Chris was feeling like a soggy towel himself. In psychosexual terms, his ego was experiencing hunger pangs, so after several tequilas, when Gina Walker told him he was the best man she'd ever been to bed with, and also one of the most creative, smartest dealmakers she'd ever worked with, Chris couldn't resist.

I believe that Gina had not set out deliberately to seduce Chris. What happened was a clear-cut, simple example of unmet needs that lead to infidelity.

What, specifically, had Gina done to meet Chris's needs? As they hadn't finished up their business conversation and it was dinnertime, she offered to cook at home. Gina, as I was to find out, was a terrific chef, so it was typical of her to ask him over instead of going to a restaurant. She had jokingly interrogated him about what his favorite dish was. He'd told her meat loaf was his passion, and sure enough meat loaf, candles, and plenty of good California pinot noir were on the table when they sat down to eat. A special meal: cooked *just for him*. To put it on a very primitive psychological level: The child in Chris was being fed. The child felt Gina truly cared for him and his well-being.

Then, over dinner, as they were discussing deals, she listened avidly to him. She asked questions, discovered the difficulties of his work, the slams he'd been taking trying to make a name for himself in New York. She responded by comforting him and reminding him of how terrific and clever he'd been at the deals they'd done together in the past, and how creative and inventive his thinking was on the project they were now working on. I have no doubt that she was sincere in her praise. But it was more than appreciation she was showing. She was feeding him where he was famished—emotionally. His need to feel powerful, to have achieved something, was being validated by Gina. The mature man was aware that she was proud of him, approved of him.

To top things off, when they began to reminisce about the past, she made sure she let him know he'd been the "best lover." The adolescent in him was gratified—for the moment at least—that he was the object of her whole sexuality. He felt sexually skillful, powerful, a real man.

Gina was nurturing Chris on all three psychosexual levels: child, adolescent, adult male; and he, in response, perceived her as understanding, warm, and sensitive to him—in a word, he found her desirable. The only trouble was she wasn't his girlfriend. The girlfriend was three thousand miles away, unaware of the fact that Chris had reached the perilous point where the psychosexual dynamic of unmet needs had swung into action—action that took place on Gina Walker's pink-canopied Posturepedic. I was determined *never* to let that happen to me again.

TWELVE

How to Get Your Man to Be Monogamous

Now you know the basic strategy to monogamy—
feed-the-ego—but how, exactly, do you go about
achieving this abstract concept in a concrete way in your
own intimate relationship?

You've already taken the first step: You've become
aware of the hungry ego—both his and yours. You
understand his basic ego needs: conquest, achievement,
sex, power; and you recognize yours: love, loving and
being loved.

The second step is finding out what your particular man
requires on a daily basis for care and feeding of his ego.
In order to find out exactly what nutrients will work most
effectively, you need EMPATHY.

Empathy is the capacity to participate in another person's feelings or ideas, the ability to vividly conceive
what the other person is loving, hating, fearing, anxious
about, and comfortable with. If you imagine how he
thinks and feels, then you can more clearly pinpoint what
his specific needs are.

"Empathy means seeing the world from the perspective of the other person," says Karl Scheibe, professor of psychology at Wesleyan University, who conducts classes in which students dramatically act out the roles of others in order to get into their skins. Most people lack confidence about their empathic power, he says. "You probably already know more than you think you know about the other person."

"The enemy of empathy is antagonism," adds Dr. Scheibe. Be aware that old conflicts and quarrels interfere with an empathic response. In order to have empathy work successfully for you, you must *want* to be empathetic, he emphasizes.

Because of our interactions with others, most of us bring a certain quantity of empathy to any relationship. But the wattage of insight into another person, specifically your husband or lover, can be amplified if you first recognize and accept a basic characteristic that most men possess—*they do not communicate well about their needs.*

Listening to the Silent Sex

By now your brain has been grooved with this idea: Sex and its elemental linkage with power, conquest, and achievement is core, critical, consistent, and constant in most men's lives.

But what about other needs your specific mate may have? How can you find out about them? Ask him, would be the most obvious answer to that one. Talking can help tremendously to develop empathy and to find out what needs are—yours and his. But most men won't talk. Especially about needs.

To be empathetic with a man, you first should know why he won't talk. Have you ever noticed that a man may look as if he's hot under the collar when you want to "have a little discussion" with him? He actually may be. Many men undergo actual physiological changes when they're faced with "talking about it": Pulse rates and heartbeats increase and they feel a surge of anxiety. In contrast, recent research points out, women are more comfortable with verbal exchanges, we take words more literally (e.g., he says, "I'll talk to you later." You wait for the phone call that evening but to him, his words are just a social sign-off) and we feel more at ease when talking about intimate/emotional issues.

"You're asking me about understanding a man's needs, but you've got to grasp his mechanism, first," says Larry Jansen, a writer friend of mine. "A man's got emotions, but he's awkward with them. He's a baby in an area that he considers women very grown-up in. Give us a chance. It takes time to reach the emotional level of most females. It takes time for us to learn to communicate."

Most men aren't as articulate as Larry. Very often when I talked to a man about talking, I could almost see the mental windshield wipers going. Men were in heavy weather with this kind of questioning and, because they wouldn't talk about it, I was not exactly clear about what the problem was, and I realized Larry had only touched the surface of the issue.

I felt I needed to do further groundwork on men's re-luctance to verbalize when it comes to intimate areas, especially the area of needs. In short, I wanted addi-tional information on the subject in order to have more empathy myself, so I called Robert Lang, my long-time research assistant. Robert is twenty-eight, holds a Ph.D. from Columbia University, writes and teaches, and has been involved with this monogamy project as well as my last two books. "I need to know why men don't talk, Robert," I said airily, as he dropped by my office to go over the kinds of material I was looking for.

Rather than our usual banter about monogamy research,

he sat down immediately, removed his horn-rimmed glasses and rubbed the lenses with a piece of tissue. I waited for him to ask what documentation I needed, but instead he said, "A man's private life is where the weak spots are; it's the underbelly of his existence."

He stopped.

"Tell me more," I said. "This is exactly the kind of thing men don't talk about."

"Intimacy or the closest kind of connection," he continued, putting on his glasses, "refers to emotional vulnerability and men can't be vulnerable. Our society still discourages it. To discuss intimacy, to discuss your relationship with someone, is to declare your own state, who you are. It's also declaring a need and men aren't supposed to have needs."

"But Robert," I interrupted, "you're twenty-eight, surely you don't buy that—how else can I put it?—macho stuff? Surely your generation has come further than that."

"That's exactly my point, we haven't," he replied. "Men still are supposed to be independent. They can talk about sex because it is pleasure and technique, conquest, power, game. They don't want to discuss intimacy because they don't want to admit they need anything or anybody. A discussion on relationships or intimacy or monogamy is a reminder to men of their lacks and of the fact that they do need people, they are dependent."

I recognized immediately that Robert had beautifully delivered the answer to why men don't like to talk about intimate areas of their lives. To put his words a little differently: Anxiety and/or fear of appearing inadequate are the real roots of a man's unwillingness to say what he needs. If he's inadequate, he may be rejected, so his thinking goes. Rejection can be painful, if not devastating, thus, better not to talk about such touchy issues as needs.

Fine-tuning Your Eyes and Ears

Your brain should by now be tattooed with the generic male ego requisites—and you more fully understand why men don't talk about them. Now, how are you to get a fix on *your* lover's specific brand of needs? The answer is not complex: You become a sensitive and meticulous observer of your mate.

Can you answer the following questions?

How does he react when you give him a compliment?

How does he respond if you offer him coffee or orange juice in bed?

How does he feel if you ask him about his work?

Do you know when he needs time/space for himself?

Do you know what his favorite sexual fantasies are?

What are his personal signs of stress?

Do you know the moments when he feels dispirited or depressed? Do you know why he's feeling that way?

If he's not interested in sex, do you know why?

Can you assess—accurately—the degree of stress that he might be feeling?

What's his reaction to sexy underwear ads? to *Playboy?*

If he pays the bills, do you know what runs through his mind as he does them?

What would he do if you brought home an X-rated video?

I posed these same questions to most of the men I interviewed, and a surprising number said that they felt that their mates wouldn't *really* know the answers.

The questions above are just to get you started thinking about what you should be finding out, if you don't already know it, about your husband or lover. You want to know as accurately as possible what he loves, likes, dislikes, detests, and what he wants, thinks, feels, fantasizes about.

Counsels one well-known psychologist, "Find out what the other person values. Ask him and also watch carefully what kinds of reward—or deprivation—he responds to." In short, what you're aiming for is unearthing everything you can about him so that you will be more able to see the world through his lenses.

An important part of the meticulous observing and sleuthing that leads to great empathy is undiluted *listening*. When investigators at Yale University rated what counted most in a close relationship, the top two clusters were communication and support followed by understanding and appreciation.

"In placing the highest value on communication and support," says Robert Sternberg of this study conducted with Sandra Wright and reported in *The Triangle of Love*, "people show they want somebody who can not only communicate effectively how he or she feels but also listen attentively."

"If you want to make a major improvement in your relationship in a minimum of time," Dr. Sternberg stresses, "try listening carefully to what your partner says, and—equally important—show your empathy by putting yourself in his or her place."

A woman who recently moved to Tenants Harbor, Maine, had some sage comments on the idea of observing and listening to the male of the species in order to uncover his needs.

"You get to Maine," she told me from the phone in her kitchen, "and you see two mallard ducks on your front porch, happy and contented in the sunshine, and you take the time to watch them, to listen to their silence. Men and woman in New York as well as every other pressured city don't take time to listen and to watch. Stillness is absolutely essential to learning how to see and how to listen and how to decipher.

"Many women are so busy telling men what to think,

what to do—to be monogamous, for example—that they don't listen. Most women spend a lot of time talking but not hearing what men say. We were raised to tell our dolls what to say and I think we often transfer that notion to men. Men are not dolls, they're grown-ups with their own thoughts. Give them time to express them, either in words or actions, and you'll find out a great, great deal about them."

Listen when he's talking with you. Listen when he talks to his colleagues, his cronies, his friends, his parents. Listening is an invaluable tool as it accomplishes three important things at once:

• Listening is an effective means to discover his needs.

• Listening raises your empathy quotient.

• Listening is a remarkably simple way to nourish his ego.

My own experience with listening provides a good example of how these three aspects can work for you. Every time I explain to a man that I'm asking questions in order to hear *his* side, *his* point of view, and that I have *ample time* to really listen to what is being said, I receive a very different response from when I simply declare, "This is what I'd like to interview you about." As soon as I let a man know that I'm genuinely interested in what he has to say, he begins to feel that he has something significant to offer, which he does—every human being does. The psychosexual dynamic of ego needs swings into action: He feels that he's important (his ego is being nourished)—which I sincerely believe he is—and thus, he's more inclined to feel better about himself and me. His ego has been given a little boost and I, in return, am also rewarded by a more thoughtful, more sincere, more revealing interview.

When I talk with a man, I want to make him feel as if I am trying to look out from his spectacles with his particular astigmatism in mind and, as I said, for my purposes, it works. He feels good and I get what I want. In my case it's strictly business, but the logic applies to every male-female relationship.

Repatterning

So far you've taken the following steps to monogamy:

- become aware of a man's ego needs

- recognized the necessity of feeding the ego

- understood that most men are miserable communicators when it comes to what satisfies their ego appetites

- observed, carefully listened to him, asked yourself questions about his ego needs, and learned how your man reacts to specific stimuli to his ego

- developed the all-important ability to empathize

The next step to be taken is what I've called *repatterning*. Once you're aware of the principle of feed-the-ego and you've become empathetic, you want to repattern your thinking and your reactions so that you are meeting his needs—and your own—on an ongoing basis.

If you decide to stage a "feed-the-ego" evening replete with everything your man desires from his most favorite meat loaf to wearing your prettiest nightgown, that's fine and good, but it's not what I'm talking about. You have to be aware of feed-the-ego in your life day by day. This means being sensitive to your man's sexual and emotional temperature and any changes they may register. Grand gestures like weekends away or stolen afternoons in a hotel making love to him are delicious, but they aren't the bread and butter of monogamy. What you're aiming for is repatterning your thinking and behavior to apply the feed-the-ego strategy, to make it part of your automatic response system.

As you observe him facing the stresses of the office, the bills, the in-laws, the rejections—as well as the joys of everyday life—think of what is going on with ego needs rather than your usual reaction to what has happened. Assess the state of his ego, and then look for ways to nourish it on a simple, everyday basis. This can take the form of bringing him a cup of steaming coffee in bed in the morning if that's what gives him pleasure and makes him feel that he's king of the roost, or it can be something even less time-consuming. "I put Crest on his toothbrush at night," one woman told me. "I had done it the night we first slept together and he really liked that—it became a love symbol for him."

My friend Claire provides a good illustration of paying attention to ego needs and then repatterning her reactions based on what she's observed. She doesn't deliver coffee or orange juice (she did, however, once bake a seductive lemon cream pie) but in her case, feeding her lover's ego takes a different, yet extremely simple, form.

Claire has been living with an exciting, highly sucessful, dynamic man for a year and a half and is herself a high-profile business personality in New York. We have ongoing discussions about my monogamy research and we'd been talking about the feed-the-ego principle when she called me one afternoon.

"You know I think Bill is one of the two or three most intelligent men I have ever met, and I have run into plenty of smart guys," she began, "I can't be gushy and

I don't drop random compliments. I assume Bill is aware of how terrific I think he is—otherwise, why would I be with him?"

Before I could respond, she went on, "Listen to this. Last weekend we managed to get away without the children and without work. We started talking about a sticky business thing he'd been involved in and I told him, 'You really are smart. The way you handled that deal you just described was brilliant.' You won't believe his reaction!"

"Tell me," I said, smiling.

"The direct sexuality in his response was instantaneous. He said, 'You really think that? Because if you do, I'm about to attack you right this minute.' We had a pretty terrific time that afternoon. . . . That one comment made me see I'd been making a serious mistake by not telling him how much I admire his work and how proud I am of him."

I once again recalled Dr. Train's words, "A woman must recognize that her mate is part boy, part adolescent, part man. The boy in him wants to know that she cares for him and his well-being. The adolescent wants to know that he's the object of her whole sexuality, the mature man wants to know that she's proud of him, approves of him. In essence it's a continuous nurturing process throughout life. What keeps us together is nurturing of each other's ego needs."

What Claire had done was to take note of Bill's reaction to a simple but sincere compliment, and it made her realize she'd administered a highly effective dose of ego vitamins. The nourishment paid off in several ways; his self-esteem was reinforced, his self-confidence was energized and so was his libido. Claire's ego needs were immediately and generously satisfied by more affection, more intimacy—and some great sex—from her simple but perfectly aimed remark.

From that experience, Claire became aware that Bill needs small but continuing shots of knowing that she feels he's a pretty terrific guy. She had assumed that he knew she found him wonderful. In fact, he needs to be reminded openly—and regularly—that she believes he's smart and wonderful and sexy.

. In the past year, Claire has repatterned her thinking and her reactions to Bill. She restyled her responses to meet his ego needs. She now tells him he's terrific or brilliant when he's made a move that she admires or respects. She's not being "gushy" and she's never insincere because it's not in her nature to be anything but direct and honest. What she's done is repatterned her behavior to be a lot more aware and much more verbal about telling Bill what he needs to hear.

"At first I thought he would think I was overdoing it," she told me. "It seemed so obvious to say, 'That was great, you're terrific,' but he responded every time by being more affectionate and paying much more attention to me. I can't deny that the feed-the-ego thing is amazingly effective."

"I was skeptical," says a woman from Minneapolis with whom I'd discussed the idea of feed-the-ego during a long interview, "but I tried an experiment and it worked. For years my husband wanted me to be home on Saturday afternoons when he finished his golf game. Saturday is a precious day for me. I get errands done for the kids and organize my life for the next week, so I never really took him seriously.

"I have a friend who drops everything when her husband gets home from golf. She's even gone so far as to lie stark naked on a fur rug in front of the fireplace when he walks in the door. They have a terrific marriage, and I know he's monogamous and crazy about her after fourteen years. Well, I figured she was meeting his 'ego needs' in a very basic way and I'd take a cue from her.

The Playmate number is definitely not my style, but one Saturday I decided to leave the kids at Grandma's, put on the sexiest negligee I own, and which I haven't worn for years, and see what happened. If nothing else we'd get a good laugh out of it because J.D., my husband, has a great sense of humor. Surprise! He was turned on by the whole scene. Next surprise: I did the same thing the following Saturday and the one after that. It worked each time. He took me to a romantic restaurant for dinner. He even bought me perfume!

"Now I really do pay attention to the details of his activities and his moods and his reactions. In return, I'm well rewarded. He is really affectionate and romantic. . . . He may get turned on by one of the secretaries in the office—he's only human—but for sure he's not going to do anything about it now that I've got his number."

So—what does it take to get *your* man's number? My advice is simply this:

1. Understand that his ego is hungry for sex, power, and achievement.

2. Make a conscious, deliberate choice to feed that ego.

3. Listen, empathize, and repattern your thinking and your behavior to fulfill those ego needs.

4. Be terrific in bed. (Specifics on how-to in the following pages.)

5. Remember that your own hungry ego will be amply nourished and rewarded if you follow the above.

THIRTEEN

Love Passages

There are a number of phases or stages that each couple traverses as they try to forge an intimate relationship over time. Most of the therapists and marriage counselors I talked with divided the developmental aspects of a relationship into four basic phases which I've labeled Razzle-Dazzle, Who Is This Person? Acknowledgment, and, finally, I Accept. These "love passages" need some exploration in order to pinpoint more precisely how, when, and where to feed the ego—both sexually and emotionally.

One: Razzle-Dazzle

You're madly in love. In fact you're both dazzled by what's happening. Sex is incredible. You spend weekends in bed. The hours fly by as you talk together about everything under the sun. You write notes, give gifts. You see him as marvelous, a true soul mate, an unbelievable find. You tell your friends how terrific he is and what wonderful attributes you're discovering in each other. All the clichés apply, you're in love and it's the best thing that ever happened. . . . *This is infatuation.*

One of the men I interviewed summed up this stage and the passage into the next when he told me, "When I was younger I used to experience the feeling of being in love quite frequently. But I don't think that being in love, in the sense that is usually accepted by the culture, is a healthy state. I mean the infatuation is with an image rather than a real person. It is very much like being a satellite in the gravitational field of a planet, and one is not running on his own strength. Two people in love are looking at their own reflections in the mirror. They are not looking at individual people. I know the feeling because if a woman is in love with me—I mean infatuated with me—I feel uncomfortable. There are expectations which I will not be able to fulfill because I am real."

In his treatise *De l'Amour*, Stendhal named the process that occurs during the infatuation stage *crystallization*, after a phenomenon observed in the mines of Austria. Crystallization turns a bare tree branch into an object of salt-encrusted beauty, as it turns a mere person into an object of intense erotic love.

The Razzle-Dazzle stage can last as long as a few days or weeks or even up to a year or more, depending on the couple. During this period they may be seeing a great deal of each other or even living together. In this time ego needs are usually not a problem because they are being met easily. A man feels he has "won" a wonderful woman, his ego is enhanced by his own projections of what she is, he thrives on the sexual relationship— and he feels fulfilled. It's easy to see how a woman's primary ego needs are met in this phase: She is in love, her ego feels immensely gratified by the affection, warmth, and sexual attention she is receiving—and giving. "Both egos are fed almost automatically as they draw upon the narcissistic aspects of the infatuation stage," is the way one psychotherapist outlined this period of a relationship.

Many relationships never progress further than the intoxication of Razzle-Dazzle or the captivation of crystallization. As soon as the lover shows the slightest signs of being a real person, not the projection of your imagination or your unconscious fantasies, trouble may not be far behind and the relationship will end.

"Realities [in the infatuation phase] model themselves enthusiastically on one's desires," proclaims Stendhal, and he is correctly identifying those "narcissistic" properties of Razzle-Dazzle. The next phase of a relationship, however, brings another kind of reality directly into the picture.

Two: Who Is This Person?

In this stage of a love relationship, the real person shows through the glamour and glitz. Who is this man? you wonder. What does he mean by leaving a nasty ring in the bathtub? Why does he call at six-thirty to ask "What are the plans for this evening?" when you'd settled it last night that you'd meet at the movies at seven. And why does he now have to visit his parents every week when it was never so necessary before? And who is the person who isn't so wonderfully romantic as he was and even leaves greasy plates to pile mile high in the sink when he used to be so wonderfully scrupulous about stacking them in the dishwasher?

One of the women I spoke with framed this phase with these words: "I'd been seeing Stuart for about a year very seriously and I was wildly in love with him. He was the perfect man for me. He had everything in megabytes: brains, wit, true sensitivity—and he was a really terrific lover. . . . One night he told me that it was hard for him to sleep next to me because my body radiated heat and it made him uncomfortable. I was terribly hurt and disturbed. Why hadn't he told me that before? A few weeks after that we had several debates about politics, which we both feel strongly about. Suddenly they weren't discussions but real arguments. I realized he's a lawyer and he's got to make his point, no matter what. He really made me angry. While we were arguing about what I thought was some insignificant political detail, I was standing in the kitchen and I had the strangest feeling wash over me: Who is this man really? I wondered. What am I arguing about? who am I arguing with? why am I here?''

Razzle-Dazzle has given way. Reality is setting in. The infatuation is over. The tree branch is bare of its beautiful, glittering salt crystals. You have to deal with who your mate is, not what you imagined him to be.

This phase in a relationship may take anywhere from a few weeks to many months. Some therapists claim that this period lasts from initial meeting until about two years. The majority of couples in this stage are living together, but that's not necessarily a prerequisite to make it to—or through—this phase. In any case, it is precisely here where disillusion and disenchantment seep into the relationship as each member of the couple must make major readjustments in their perceptions of one another.

And it is here that the ego becomes more aware of its hunger, but its cries for far more substantial fare cannot be verbalized or even clearly recognized because real intimacy and the communication that it engenders has not yet had time to form.

Thus, this is a most dangerous phase because the bonding between you is still so fragile and ruptures come so easily and without apparent explanation.

Three: Acknowledgment

This is the stage when you find yourself making statements like: "Oh yes, that's how he is. He'll pick up the towels, but there's no way he's going to throw them in the hamper." Or "I know that he won't talk when something's bothering him and it makes me crazy." Or "He wants sex when he's under stress, but he can't understand why I'm just not interested." Or "There he goes again, he's told that one three times already—but I won't remind him of it."

If you have reached this third stage, you are probably living together and will almost certainly have experienced disappointments and restless, unsettled feelings. On the other hand once you've relinquished the rose-colored glasses of Razzle-Dazzle and have recognized your mate for a real person, you'll begin to understand who he is—a mortal, like you, with all kinds of characteristics, good and not so very good. It's in this phase where you have much more accurately targeted his ego needs—and your own—and you are beginning to know how to satisfy them in ways that are specific to each of you individually.

Here, too, timing is difficult to project. This phase of acknowledgment of the multidimensional reality of the other person can take two or three months to about a year and a half to work through. But the comprehension and awareness you've gained are the keys to the riches of the following phase: acceptance. In this next period you're in a position to link together to form a third entity—an intimate, long-lasting relationship.

Four: I Accept

"From the very first date, I knew there were good things and bad things about him. I never hid them from myself. I wanted to be with him more than anything, but one of the hardest parts was—still is, and probably always will be—abiding and accepting those bad things." These words from a woman who has been happily and monogamously married for eleven years characterize the last and ongoing period of an intimate relationship—acceptance.

This is the mature phase of a marriage. You recognize and embrace each other as individuals. You've anticipated wet towels on the bathroom floor and they're no longer a personal insult. You're both constantly in the process of keeping intimacy alive through accepting each other as real, three-dimensional people and communicating as two individuals who possess differing needs and desires.

The delicate balancing between independence, each of you as separate entities, and intimacy, the two of you connecting physically and emotionally, has been and continues to be negotiated with a positive outcome. You accept each other—and the relationship—as it is and as it develops. To put it into other words: Both of you have gotten pretty adept at recognizing and fulfilling each other's ego needs.

If you've gotten this far, the odds are good that the relationship will evolve and ripen into one that endures. And if ego needs—both yours and his—continue to be recognized and satisfied over the swings and changes, the ups and downs, of the process of living, the chances of a monogamous relationship are very high.

FOURTEEN

The
Peril Points

Along the road of love, as we've just seen in the last chapter, you can expect to find smooth expanses, lots of potholes, and some tricky switchbacks. Chris Franklin and I had been living together for about a year and we had entered the rough route from Razzle-Dazzle to Who Is This Person? But that was not the only difficulty to be faced at that time. Unknowingly, Chris and I were to encounter Peril Point 1 at almost the same moment.

When Chris departed for the West Coast, I was relatively oblivious to his problems because I was so immersed in my own work. While I paid meager attention, the twin ego reefs of sexual and professional stress were forming an undertow that propelled Chris straight to infidelity. Although the ego is ever-needy, ceaselessly searching for morsels to maintain its strength, there are spells when it will settle for nothing less than a banquet—and that's exactly what Chris needed at that rocky period in his life. Those extra-vulnerable times in the course of a relationship when a man can so quickly clamber into the psychosexually replenishing bed of another woman are what I've identified as Peril Points.

Reality Check:
Peril Point 1

This first, classic Peril Point you will confront arrives in that intricate interstice between infatuation and the reality of intimacy—exactly where Chris and I were. In other words, Peril Point 1 occurs during the already jarring passage between Razzle-Dazzle and Who Is This Person? It's here that he's wondering if it's love he really feels and does he want to progress further into a relationship with a person who is less an ideal and more a real human being. As he's grappling with this, he looks around and sees other women who still glisten with the allure of razzle-dazzle, with whom sex is easy—and there are no apparent problems to plague him.

As the relationship grows less idyllic and more difficult to deal with, Peril Point 1 rises to its peak. In her important and influential book, *Intimate Partners* (Random House, 1987), Maggie Scarf puts this idea into perspective: "The lower the evaluation of a relationship, and the lower the frequency and quality of the sex with the spouse, the more likely was it that extramarital sex would occur. This is why, even though the timing of any extramarital romantic fling or affair cannot be foretold, the phase of disillusionment and disenchantment—when disappointment and restlessness are prominent—is one during which sexual acting out is much likelier to happen. Not only is infidelity more probable during this period, but the betrayal of the bond will feel most justified."

"Monogamy comes easiest in the first or second year," says psychiatrist Anthony Pietropinto. Sex, he explains, is the glue that holds a couple together while they're exploring each other and passing into the second, jolting, Who Is This Person? phase.

But a double danger is occurring at this period. Dreams and fantasies are fading as reality comes into sharp and sometimes disagreeable focus—and it is often at just about this same time that the delicious novelty of sex is beginning to wear off.

It's exactly here, at Peril Point 1, that the lure of infidelity can be irresistible. The reason: Unmet needs, which had been camouflaged behind the dazzle of infatuation, begin to surface. And with the entrance of these unsatisfied needs, the desire for psychosexual gratification soars—the ego is hungrier than ever.

It's at this classic Peril Point that the sexual relationship must remain vital because it can be a safe harbor to return to while each of you questions whether to proceed to the next phase. Making love, and the intimacy it renews, is the bonding stuff of a relationship during this period. As he begins to realize that he must adjust and address his fears of intimacy and "entrapment," his ego requires plenty of reinforcement. He needs to reconfirm his own sense of maleness, his power, and his independence, and sex is one of the most immediate and effective ways for him to accomplish this. To put it in other words: Good sex at home during Peril Point 1 is critically important.

Peril Point 1 is particularly hazardous and pernicious, but the issue of monogamy for a man will be an ongoing concern and a fairly constant interior conflict unless he receives that requisite care and nourishment of his emotional and sexual needs. However, despite the best intentions, despite vigilance and understanding, there will be other situations, other Peril Points, where the ego exacts gourmet treatment to keep it from dining out elsewhere.

More Peril Points

Extraordinary stress at work—for either one of a couple—
is also a standard Peril Point. "You'd think the last thing
I would be able to do was screw around under the circumstances," says a law student who was preparing to
take the bar exam and who works full-time as a parale-
gal during the day. "I have a great girlfriend; we've been
living together for three years, and I know she'd go nuts
if she thought I made it with another woman. But I did.
I was so wiped out at the library one night that I had a
stress screw with a woman who was in one of my classes
and was studying for the bar too. It was a way to get
rid of piled-up tension. Why didn't I go home? Because
my girlfriend was too busy working on her own thesis.
We hadn't had a chance to have sex in four days, and
I definitely need more than that when I'm in deep
waters."

This story represents something of an extreme, but it
is useful in understanding a man's mind-set. This man
was twenty-four, an age at which sexuality is close to its
peak intensity for males. His needs, both physical and
emotional, were bearing down hard and his student status afforded him the opportunity of being near a group
of willing and available young women who were under
similar duress.

The majority of men that I interviewed who were unfaithful during particularly strained periods cannot, on
a moment's notice, so easily locate an obliging female.
But, as we've seen, they can promptly develop work-
oriented liaisons, and that all-too-common phenomenon,
the "office affair," is the obvious consequence of not
taking cognizance of this Peril Point.

The birth of a child is a classic situation where a man can
feel ignored, neglected, and rejected. A thirty-four-year-

old physician from Stamford, Connecticut, put the problem simply: "My wife was breast-feeding," he says. "I had been made aware of possible feelings of rejection, and obviously I knew that hormonal changes make women relatively uninterested in sex during the lactation period. But I felt really put off. I thought somehow that I'd failed. There I was wanting to have my sexuality confirmed. I needed a woman to reconfirm me for the decent, responsible guy I am. I knew it was wrong, I knew I was having a problem, that I was being selfish and irrational, but three months after the baby was born, I went to bed with one of the nurses at the hospital."

At a symposium on love, sex, and marriage for *Ladies' Home Journal* in March 1988, sociologist and author (*American Couples*, with Philip Blumstein, William Morrow & Co., 1983), Pepper Schwartz addressed the same issue. The panel had been discussing the physiological basis for a woman's lack of sexual desire after childbirth. "I wanted sex sooner than my husband," declared Schwartz. "Why? Because I wanted to keep my marriage intact. My mind overruled my hormones and I had real sexual desire even though I was nursing my first child."

A couple I know who had a child four months ago adheres to the doctrine that their marriage comes above all else. Both have high-stress work situations—and Diane is nursing and hopes to continue for at least two more months. The second week after Jeremy was born, Diane and Mike resumed their "Wednesday nights," the time they'd set aside since they first met to go out for a quiet dinner at a neighborhood restaurant so they can be alone together in an intimate way. "The babysitter is reserved for every Wednesday. The only adjustment we make in this plan is the time we leave the apartment, as Jeremy's feeding schedule is still unsettled," says Diane.

What is actually taking place during these intimate dinners is an acknowledgment and replenishment of Mike's ego supplies. Even though she has far less time to meet her husband's psychosexual requirements, he derives enough nourishment during this admittedly difficult period from having her complete and undivided attention if only for a few hours.

Failure and/or rejection Being hit hard, defeated, foiled, or frustrated—these are obvious and definitive Peril Points. Rare is the man—or woman—whose ego doesn't take a beating from failure or rejection. Some of us are more resilient than others, but for most humans, it's pretty tough to hear that you've been turned down for a job, that the raise you thought you deserved isn't forthcoming, that your ideas for a new project aren't even being considered, that you haven't been invited to come to the party—whatever or wherever it might be, figuratively or literally. The ego can be instantly depleted and sorely deflated by that kind of treatment, and it needs filling up as soon and as often as possible in order for it to recover.

Mid-life crisis "I've solved my mid-life crisis by getting a new job, not a girlfriend," joked a friend of mine when we were discussing Peril Points. "Nothing made any sense to me. I began to question everything I was doing," said a forty-one-year-old man who was in the throes of replotting his life when I talked with him. "I'd been monogamous, but I wanted to see what it was like to have sex with another woman. I was obsessed with the idea that I couldn't go to my grave without having sex with someone else. None of this had anything to do with my wife. It was something that was going on inside me."

"Was there anything she could have done that would have stopped you from being unfaithful?" I asked.

"No, absolutely not. She was doing everything right. You were talking about needs—she was meeting all my needs, sexually, emotionally, etcetera. But this was a need that she couldn't possibly have met. It had nothing to do with her. It was an interior problem. Mine and mine alone."

What he's describing is typical of mid-life crisis and the "identity" quagmire that ensues. "Who am I now?" is one of the basic issues that this man was wrestling with during this period. Very often a man feels the question can best be answered through sex. This should come as no surprise if you recall how completely masculine identity is equated with sex and sexuality. Being a man means being sexual. Thus, many men sail through a mid-life crisis by becoming involved with a younger woman, divorcing a wife, taking a mistress, experimenting with a new sexual geometry. This kind of sexual acting-out doesn't solve any of his problems, but it's a familiar and expedient means of trying to reestablish who he is and where he's going.

The wife or lover of a man who is thrashing about in the deep waters of mid-life crisis can help—but only in a limited way. The man quoted above is correct, it's *his* problem and only he can solve it.

"Discussing a man's desire to have sex with another woman can sometimes effectively defuse the urge to be unfaithful. Acknowledging these needs can help alleviate his anxiety and reaffirm who he is," counsels a psychotherapist. "But the most important thing for a woman to remember is that if a man does have sex outside the relationship during this critical period, she shouldn't overreact and feel that she is responsible. I know that sounds easy to say, but if she wants to maintain the relationship, she's got to try and understand what's going on. If there's ever a time when she has to comprehend and meet his needs, it's this one and it's the toughest."

A detailed analysis of infidelity, identity, and mid-life crisis is outside the scope of this book, but if you are at this Peril Point in a relationship, the wisest course of action is to seek the advice of a competent marriage counselor or psychotherapist who is trained in working with couples.

Success! You might assume that a prerequisite for, or a by-product of, professional or personal triumph is a hardy ego, one that is flourishing, well-fed, and fit. You would think that the primal male need for conquest, power, and achievement has been adequately met when a man is successful in an endeavor that's meaningful to him. You might further conclude that such accomplishments would lead a normally monogamous man to turn to his mate to celebrate and share the spoils.

Assume no such thoughts. Where success is concerned, quite often the reverse holds true.

The sort of success under discussion here is not the immediate short-term variety—shooting an under par game, performing a skillful procedure. It's the feat that's taken time and energy to achieve that, ironically, can lead to eventual infidelity. A man who's just been made partner or vice president, or won an election or a bronze medal, or has realized recognition after years of toil and hardship often anoints his victory with another woman or a series of them. Why?

The answer, once again, lies in the ego. Do I really deserve this dessert? the ego very often asks. It tasted so very good, I'm in a hurry for more. But am I worthy of it all? I got what I hungered for, but I'm really worried now—can I be successful again?

A man whom I interviewed who had been monogamous during an uphill climb to the top of a management consulting firm told me, "I have always believed in hard work, ethics—and being faithful. And I truly considered myself happy with my wife. For eleven years I've been working toward having my own business so I could live the kind of life Joanna and I have dreamed of. We'd take trips, enjoy the theatre and the arts, we'd be able to get together and do the things that we've never had time for.

"I've always traveled a great deal on business, and never once during a decade have I been unfaithful, although I had plenty of opportunity. But after I was 'successful' and had my own firm, I began to play around. Why? Because the pressure to maintain the business was so intense, the competition was so cutthroat that I constantly felt I would go under.

"My wife didn't seem to understand this but Kim, who happened to be my colleague, did. Kim just listened to all my problems and kept reassuring me that I would always be on top. Down deep I really didn't believe that, but at least it was better than the complaints from my wife about how I hadn't lived up to what I promised when I 'made it.' I never had any intention of being unfaithful, but I found myself having an affair with Kim after my wife left on a vacation by herself. Joanna and I had planned on taking that trip together, but a real crisis came up at work and I could not take the time off. Joanna simply did not understand. But Kim did."

Joanna did not recognize the fact that as her husband had reached his long-sought-after goal, he was facing a possible Peril Point. She herself had worked so long and hard with him to achieve that success that she did not see the fallout and perceive the consequences—which were that his psychosexual needs increased as the pressures on him escalated, even though those pressures were positive ones.

There are many Peril Points to monogamy in any love relationship. The ones described above are perhaps the most common you'll encounter but there will be other, less definitive moments and periods of strain. The idea to keep in mind is that you want to develop your awareness and perception of when your lover is facing exceptional difficulties and know that these are the times when the ego is ravenous and insists on even more than its regular care and feeding.

There are three distinct signals that should help to warn you of an approaching Peril Point. They are

• Lower Frequency of Sex

Let's say you've been making love two or three times a week or once a week and this pattern changes and you find yourself pleading a migraine or he falls asleep in five seconds flat; pay special attention to what's happening in other areas of your life. Are one or the other—or both of you—under special strain at work or at home? How were the last few times you made love? Could he be having a problem with performance that he's afraid to talk about?

Sexual frequency in a marriage is not constant. Studies have shown that lovemaking falls off after the first year or two, but a pattern that is satisfying *to both of you* is what's considered healthy. This pattern may be once a month or twice a day, and of course even this will vary through the ups and downs of a relationship, but the warning signal of an impending Peril Point is a real fall-off of sexual intercourse with no apparent explanation.

• Lower Quality Sex

If you remember a time when the two of you were totally in sync sexually and lovemaking was a truly intimate emotional and physical exchange, and things feel a little different now, you're experiencing lower quality sex. As with frequency, the quality and intensity of sex will, of course, vary. Sometimes you'll want to make long leisurely love and sometimes you'll want to have a "quickie," but if the quality of sexual relations falls off into a perfunctory wham-bam, or if you have the feeling that he's just not "there," then pay heed. If you find yourself worrying about the bills or performing in a rote way—or you sense that's what's happening to him— then a possible Peril Point is at hand.

• Lower Estimation of Your Relationship

If either of you begins to take each other for granted, you can bet that you're devaluing your relationship. To put it another way, if you're not making the "relationship" a priority in your life, if you're not working at it to guard it, you'll find yourselves wandering emotionally—and sexually. If you're less committed to spending time together or you don't make an effort to find time to be alone despite work and family demands, you're heading for trouble.

A new job, a new child, new responsibilities, the death of a parent—all these real difficulties can pull you away from the core intimacy of a strong, healthy, satisfying relationship. And any of these can subtly begin to erode the value you assign to that relationship. Once you start working late, paying less attention to the two of you— for any reason—it's a sure signal that you're about to meet with a Peril Point.

The three warning signals—lower frequency of sex, lower quality sex, and lower evaluation of the relationship—should ring alarm bells. They indicate that something is wrong, that the ego needs nourishing, that psychosexual needs are not being met.

One More Point

Two final words are required on the issue of needs:
needs change.

Although the basic ego requisites of sex, power, achievement, and self-worth remain constant, the degree to which they must be attended to fluctuates, as we've just seen in examining Peril Points. In addition to this, individual needs change.

For example: A man may never have worried about his looks or attractiveness to women, but suddenly he begins to lose his hair or develop a paunch. He needs to be reminded that he's an appealing and sexy guy more than he did before these woes befell him.

Another example of needs changing, but this time on a deeper and more subtle level: a man has been dominating the sexual relationship, but now would like to be more passive, he'd like to be taken care of. His girlfriend responds by making more direct advances in lovemaking, by taking the initiative more often than she did in the past, by suggesting that they share sexual fantasies. Like the woman above, the empathetic ego watcher will have taken note of her man's changed point of view and she will react in ways that meet his new needs.

Peril Points as well as Love Passages are tricky to deal with, but one of the quickest—and surest—ways to diminish their danger is by making certain that your sexual life is very, very solid. The physical and emotional intimacy of sex can be the critical key to maintaining a relationship when egos are fragile and strained. "Very little heals a fractured ego better than love—or lovemaking," said a pastoral counselor I talked with, and I couldn't agree more.

FIFTEEN

How to Satisfy a Man Sexually

Fulfilling psychological and emotional needs takes knowledge, empathy, sensitivity, and repatterning. The same is true of sexual needs. When I asked men "Do you feel your wife or lover satisfies you sexually?" both monogamous and non-monogamous men agreed that there were major areas that could be improved on—a great deal.

If I asked you, "Quick! Name the three things your lover likes most when you make love," you should be able to answer that question as fast as you can recite your ABCs, but the fact is that many women can't. Even though we may know exactly what our husbands desire for dinner, we aren't nearly as sure about what satisfies their appetites in bed. If you're not meeting his sexual needs, by now you should know just how much trouble that can lead to.

Despite the plethora of solid physiological and psychological information about sex which is as nearby as our bookstores, radios, and TV sets, I was surprised to hear, in the late 1980s, men repeatedly say that women don't really know how to satisfy them sexually.

Here's what men have told me it takes to do it:

• Find Out What He Likes

By far the biggest grumble men have is that women are not paying the closest attention to what they love when making love.

"Well," you might respond, "I know he really likes oral sex, that's first on his list" or "He likes his nipples stimulated," but if you're not *positive* 1-2-3 what delights your man most, ask yourself why. And the answer, for most women, is that we never asked.

"It's too late," said Marge Jensen, a woman I interviewed in Chicago, "we've been married for years. Sex is not all that bad—it's not so terrific either—but I'd feel far too uncomfortable to talk about it now. So would my husband."

Her husband, it turned out, felt sexually frustrated, particularly after the birth of their first child, and had been non-monogamous for four years. "I love her, but she's just not interested in sex," he told me in a telephone interview. "I believe I save the marriage by having short-term affairs. I couldn't exist with Marge's level of sexuality and there seemed no point talking about it."

Marge did not have to present a ten-point agenda or even have a conversation about what Jim liked in bed. She could have posed two easy but subtle questions to her husband and probably saved a critical part of their relationship. Before we go on to those, there's one query you should avoid.

Don't ask: What do you like? What turns you on?

The answer is very likely to be "everything"—you've learned nothing specific. And it's the specifics that make the critical difference in lovemaking. (Think of it this way. You might know that he likes pasta, but is it fettucini or spaghettini he prefers, and what type of sauce is his particular favorite?— *that's* the specific knowledge you need to cook him an especially delicious meal.)

But how do you find out his real preferences if you've been married for years or if you've just begun a relationship? The answer lies in two simple questions calculated to deliver important information:

- Do you like this better than this?

- How does this feel? Is this as good?

By asking for comparisons you'll get yes or no answers which are the easiest for most males to give. It's not necessary, or even desirable, to retrieve all the intelligence material you'd like at once. Take your time, there are many different things you want to know—positions, places, pressures, positives, negatives—it will require more than a single lovemaking experience to find out. Even though you may think of yourself as shy or still uncomfortable about sex, using this simple yes/no discovery technique will reveal his most intimate preferences; and once you know them, you're fast on your way to being a sensitive—and better—lover, no matter how long you've been together.

- Understand the Importance of Technique

"A woman may have the best intentions—or the best body—in the world, but if she doesn't know how to touch or how to give good head, it's not going to feel as good as being with someone who does," candidly admits a friend of mine.

I've written three books on love, sex, and relationships and each of them accentuates sexual technique. And I want to bring this up yet again. Don't mistake making love for a God-given talent. You know instinctually how to multiply the species, but that's not lovemaking.

Lovemaking is much more than reproduction and sex, it's emotional and sensual luxury and a lot of it comes from skill that is, fortunately, easily acquired. With "other women" so plentiful, and with a man's ability to judge what's good and not so good sexually because he's probably had a few lovers before you to make comparisons, it's more essential than ever to know what you're doing.

Think of skillful sexual technique as doing exercises in the right way. You can go to the gym and give yourself a tough workout, huffing, puffing, and sweating as if you're contending for the Olympics, but if you're not doing your routines correctly, you're not doing your body any real good. If you have a careful trainer or someone who explains how to lift a weight correctly with your elbows slightly bent instead of locked straight, you're going to get far better results.

Ditto for sex. It doesn't just come naturally. If you want to be a terrific lover, you have to work on it. Use the yes/no questions to find out how you're doing in the technique department and you can also make a lovely request: *Show me how to do that, please.*

"The best woman I ever went to bed with was very sexually sophisticated," a man from Manhattan recalled. "I knew because she knew exactly the right pressure and the right stroke and the right timing that I needed on every part of my body. But she was charming as well as skillful. She said, 'Oh, show me how to do that, please' the second night we slept together—it was the best oral sex I ever had."

You can develop a terrific sexual "technique" by doing two things:

- Finding out through the yes/no questions what feels really good to him

- Remembering what I've called the Golden Rule Of Lovemaking. *DON'T do unto him as you would have him do unto you.* Your bodies are different, your musculature is different, your response times are different, your desires are different. He needs a stronger, firmer pressure on his entire body as well as his genitals; you need a lighter touch, and you usually need longer and sometimes much more delicate stimulation of the clitoris than he does of his penis.

The Golden Rule also helps to remind you that if you like your ears kissed, it doesn't necessarily follow that he finds ear-nibbling as titillating or endearing as you do; if you want your breasts to be stroked and caressed, he might prefer having his nipples slightly pinched; if you'd adore your toes being sucked, don't assume that's a turn-on for him too.

One last word on technique: It's important to know physical technique for every part of lovemaking, but it's *crucial* to oral sex—and oral sex is number one on the majority of men's lists of what they love sexually. Most men are naturally highly reluctant to tell a woman that she's not doing "it" right; the woman who really knows how to satisfy a man is a technically skillful lover—and she knows exactly how to delight him with oral sex.

- Understand the Importance of Oral Sex to Him

Why, many women have asked me, is oral sex so important to a man? Genital sex is great, men affirm wholeheartedly, but oral sex is direct stimulation of the most sensitive and responsive part of the body, and thus, it feels particularly fine.

Perhaps more importantly, oral sex is also an affirmation of his maleness. By making love to his penis, to his external symbol of masculinity, you are gratifying one of a man's deepest ego needs. By truly loving him, by loving his penis, you are also gratifying one of your own most important ego needs.

"You would do women a big favor," one man told me, "if you tell them this. Show a man that you genuinely enjoy giving oral sex, and the way to do this is to take all the time in the world with it—and do it smoothly and skillfully and lovingly. These days a lot of women seem to feel it's an obligation they have to a man. She thinks 'Well, he expects it, so I'll do it.' The point is not that a man expects it but that he really wants it. He can feel that kind of positive or negative attitude from a woman right away. Besides the intense physical pleasure it gives, it's the pleasure a woman shows when she is doing it to a man that really makes it a knockout experience."

• Do It Over and Over Again—then throw him a curve

"Find out what he likes and do it—again and again and again and again," is the blunt way a San Francisco personnel manager put it when I asked him what sexual advice he'd give to women. I checked this out with many of the other men I interviewed and they all concurred that this was first-rate counsel. "Even though a woman may know what turns her guy on, she often fails to do it," the executive said.

The man who gave me that insight explained that he believed the reason for this failure to do what she knows gives a man pleasure is that a woman thinks a man will find her boring if she repeats something sexually. "Not true if it's what really turns him on," he said.

"In a million years I wouldn't get tired of oral sex," concurs a man from Highland Park, Chicago. "That's the frosting on the cake. I wait for those licks—literally.

I like genital sex and lots of different positions, but almost every time we make love, I really want some oral sex."

Once you're tuned in to what your husband or lover's preferences are, keep in mind that repetition of them is not boring; on the contrary, it's welcomed. The woman who says to herself "Oh, he wants the same old thing tonight" is not understanding the psychosexual mechanics of pleasure.

But remember that repetition that becomes routine is deadly. One of the primary causes of lack of desire and inevitable, destructive, boredom is slipping into a routine.

Let's say, knowing that oral pleasuring is at the top of his list, you *always* start a lovemaking session with it: That's precisely the kind of unimaginative style that leads to dull, predictable sex. If his priority is the missionary position or he especially likes you on top, for example, do it often or even every time you make love, but combine it with other sensual techniques so it doesn't become routine.

Okay, now you can throw him a terrific curve. You've been having oral sex consistently when you make love. *Don't do it* for two or three times in a row.

There's sound theory behind this ploy. Psychologist Ellen Bersheid (in an article entitled "Emotion" appearing in *Close Relationships*, W. H. Freeman, 1983) postulates that emotion is experienced only as the result of interruption of stereotypical actions between partners. According to this view of the course of intimacy, it's essential that lovers experience minor interruptions so that they can recapture an awareness of their emotional involvement.

Think of it this way: If you keep doing something that he prefers, let's use oral sex as an example again, and you don't do it for two or three times in a row, he'll have a reaction. Because you've behaved unexpectedly and interrupted a pattern, he'll respond in a different way. It doesn't really matter what his reaction is—surprise, mild annoyance, dying for you to do it to him again—the point is that changing your lovemaking style is one psychologically proven way to keep that insidious devil, boredom, out of the sexual picture.

Kenneth Livingston, another clinical researcher (in an essay called "Love is a Process of Reducing Uncertainty" in *Love and Loving,* Jossey-Bass, 1980), has a similar take on the subject of repetition. He refers to love as a process of "uncertainty reduction." What he really means is that in order for love and passion—and sex—to thrive, an element of mystery is required. We should feel some degree of doubt about what will happen and when it will happen. Thus, it's no surprise that the great seducers, courtesans, and geishas have always maintained an enigmatic, provocative air about them.

One man I interviewed who was totally faithful in his second marriage, after a wildly adulterous first one, told me that his wife has her own separate bedroom. "She comes to me or I go to her," he said. "I'm never completely sure about what's going to happen with Jeanne. After fourteen years of marriage, she continues to surprise me at how extraordinary she is as a sexual mate."

• Explore His Fantasies

If we're sexually healthy, we have sexual fantasies. Fantasies can take many forms, from dreaming of a romantic lover to wearing "wicked" lingerie to absolutely anything else your imagination can conjure up. I believe fantasies are integrally tied to ego needs because they are a direct way of nurturing your own ego—to say it another way: A fantasy can give you instant ego gratification.

Let's say I have a fantasy of fabulous sex with a gorgeous stranger. The fantasy makes me feel desirable and sexy, it reaffirms my need to love and be loved—it makes my ego feel good.

When two people share fantasies—either verbally or in reality—their ego needs are being gratified on both a physical and psychosexual level. Part of satisfying a man sexually is exploring and sharing his fantasy world— and yours. Not only does sharing fantasies help to nourish egos, but it's a wonderful way to deepen and enhance intimacy, and it can be one of the most liberating, exciting aspects of making love.

It's important to keep in mind that *exploring and sharing fantasies doesn't necessarily mean acting them out.* "Fantasies should never be acted upon," warns one therapist, "unless you're *both* in *total agreement about* what's going to take place—and you totally trust each other. Acting out a sexual fantasy must be *mutually* pleasurable and I want to underscore that a high level of communication and complete trust must be well-established before you step into the world of fantasy."

• Let Him Know He's the Best Lover

If you've read this far, you understand that by letting him know he's a wonderful lover, you're feeding a primal ego requirement—the need to feel male, masculine, potent, powerful. "The reason a man asks that clichéd question 'Was it good for you?' is because *he'll* feel good about himself as a man if his prowess as a lover is confirmed," explains a sex therapist from Los Angeles.

"Yeah," confesses a computer consultant with a smile, "if I get the idea she's really turned on by me, if she's giving off that she's having a good time, then I'm going to believe that I'm pretty great in the sack—and I'll think she's great too."

The woman who lets a man know—either verbally and/or physically—that he's giving her real pleasure is also the woman who lets a man know that sex is a priority in her life. "If you ask me how to satisfy a man sexually, I'd have to say that the first thing a woman should do is make sure the guy knows that sex is real important to her," says an architectural draftsman who has been monogamous for eight years. "My wife is very sexy. She's easy with her own body and she lets me know she likes mine, even though I'm no Adonis."

You don't have to scream "I like sex" every time you see a man, but you can let him know by what you wear, how you touch, how you look at him that you're interested and that sex means a great deal in your life.

"I met two women recently," one man told me, "and all I could think of about the first one was that her job was top priority to her. We had sex together, but I didn't feel she was sexual, sexy. The second woman was not as attractive as the first, but she was a real turn-on. Her figure was a little overweight, but in the right places—and she wore those knit dresses that made me want to touch her all over. She told me she always wore suits to the office—she was a lawyer—but she wanted to be comfortable at night. It was a pretty smart way of informing me that she was interested in turning me on—and that I was more important to her than making partner."

How do you satisfy a man sexually? Here's a précis of the past pages to keep in mind:

- Find out what he likes and when, where, and how he likes it

- Be "technically" skillful

- Understand the importance of oral sex—do it well and take loads of time

- Do what he likes over and over—and then surprise him with something different

- Share his fantasies—and yours

- Make sex a priority and let him know he's the best lover

SIXTEEN

Five Sex Mistakes Most Women Make (and the Sixth Deadly Sexual Sin)

"A lot of women are making sex mistakes," one man told me bluntly when we were talking about how a woman could satisfy a man sexually.

"People always blame women for everything!" I responded rather hotly. "How many men are the greatest lovers in the world?"

"I don't have firsthand experience in that area," he said with a laugh, "but maybe it's better if I say there are still some misunderstandings that women have when it comes to sex."

"Okay, I accept that," I said.

Men will very often say things like "women don't understand about sex," "they're not interested enough," "they get too involved with emotions," "they're too passive," or, like the man above, they might say women are making "mistakes" in the sexual area.

If women are indeed in any way blundering sexually, it means we're still misunderstanding one of a man's basic ego needs and I, for one, wanted to know all about it.

"So, tell me, do you know of any sexual 'mistakes' that that you feel women are making? Can you tell me what more we women ought to know to get a man to be monogamous?" I began to ask men—both monogamous and not. Here are their enlightening answers:

Bad Timing

Taking time and making time are the two problems that come up most often as men (and women) talk about sexual problems and stumbling blocks.

Time, as we all too well know, is harder and harder to come by as children, jobs, and the bills make ever-soaring demands on us, but taking time to make love is, the experts all agree, crucial to the health of an intimate relationship.

"Before we were married, she stopped loading the dishwasher if I patted her on the bottom," says a Dallas teacher whose experience is echoed by many other American males. "Now I don't even bother to touch her, and when I'm handed the 'good crystal' I just dry—and I dry up sexually. She doesn't make time for me."

This dishwashing syndrome is nothing new in the literature. I've even written about it myself. But what surprised me was that I was still hearing about it so often today. So many men said that their wives would drop everything in order to make love before they were married and then, wham, instant accessibility was a forgotten dream, as soon as the wedding ceremony was over.

"She couldn't wait to get it. We'd be having dinner with friends, and the minute they'd leave we'd head for the bedroom or fall on the sofa," recalls another man. But all the sexual charge faded as he realized that the dishes were more important than he was, he added nostalgically and resentfully. Read his words as a prelude to infidelity and remember that gracious sexual access can do a great deal to stop it.

If making time to make love is important, equally fundamental is *taking time*. It's fascinating as well as instructive to hear men repeatedly describe women who are "great lovers" as the ones who take time.

Ironically, much has been made of the fact that men do not spend enough time making love to women, but the reverse is often the case. A man who began having an affair with a colleague that ended in divorce from his wife and eventual marriage to the other woman, explained that "when we were doing oral sex, I felt as if she wanted to do it to infinity. A moment would come when I wanted to be inside her, but she wouldn't let me and that made it even maddeningly better. Finally, we would end up together, but she took her own sweet time about it because she knew that that was a terrific turn-on for me." He went on to describe his marriage where "even though my wife and I had a lot of sex, I never had the idea that my wife wanted it to last. I let her know this wasn't good for me, but she never seemed to take it into her head how important sex was in my makeup, so it was something squeezed in between other things that had to be done. We always seemed to be racing to find out who could come first. I don't think it's shocking that I looked for slow, pleasurable, relaxed sex somewhere else."

No Action

If timing, or the lack of it, is one of the basic sex mistakes, movement is another area men are quick to point out as problematic. "I've been to bed with many, many women, about a hundred or more," an exceptionally handsome, recently divorced man from New York admitted, "and in all, only six or seven were really memorable as sexual partners."

Their secret? They all *moved*. In other words these women knew when, how, and where to be active. "It sounds like ancient history, but women still expect men to take the lead," this man continued, "and that's actually fine, but at a certain point you want her to do some of the work. If you pinned me down to numbers, I'd say at the very least forty percent of the activity should be done by the woman in an extended lovemaking session."

"Some women think men will back off if they take an active role," another man reported, "and it's true that can happen if she doesn't do it subtly or she's always doing the doing. I once slept with a woman who said directly, 'Just lie back, relax, and let me try this. . . .' It was one of the biggest turn-ons ever—especially since the 'this' was something I was really hot for."

Most men feel that it's the surprise or the unexpectedness of a woman wanting to take over that provides a particularly delicious sexual frisson, but most women find the take-control situation confusing and anxiety provoking. Many women have been justifiably concerned about tales of retreating and impotent males who had verbally embraced the "new" female sexual assertiveness. Just how active should I be? is what women are asking themselves and their therapists when it comes to sex. In a world where men seem to be in increasingly short supply, and women want and need monogamous relationships to succeed, the most realistic and effective advice is this:

If you are unclear—and a great many of us are—as to what is "too aggressive or too assertive" on the sexual front, keep the following in mind:

1. Men are being honest when they say they want women to be active sexually—but they only want this some of the time.

2. Men want to think that they, the men, are allowing women to take the lead.

The second point is subtle but critical: A woman who initiates, but at the same time lets the man feel he is ultimately calling the sexual shots, generates a feeling of power and potency in him—a feeling universally responded to by males.

"I remember one of the sexiest women I'd ever been to bed with," says a man from outside Seattle who was involved with a woman who knew exactly when to make her moves. "She wasn't particularly beautiful, just kind of easy on the eyes, but she had the knack of making me feel sexually like a Rambo. What she did was let me know she wanted sex, one of the sure signals was when she wore a pair of red fuck-me shoes, and she'd actually take me to the bedroom. Once we got there, she would unbutton her blouse or peel off her panty hose and stop right there. Completely stop. I had to take over. The combination of leading me to the well but making me work to reach the water was dynamite. It's like the stripper who leaves on nothing but the G-string. The guy feels he has to jump on stage and rip it off her. Once we got to actual sex, she'd do the same kind of number. Make moves on me and then pull back when she knew I was panting for it. These kinds of women know what plays to make—in bed and out—to make the guy really hot. A woman like that lets a man feel he's directed the whole scenario when in truth she's been the one who's written the script."

The Surrender Switch

Not understanding or subscribing to the "surrender switch" is another sexual "mistake" a great many women make. The idea of surrender is one instinctively understood by the kind of sexy, exciting woman just described above.

In bygone days women surrendered to men, they gave up their hearts, their souls, their virginity. A man may crave a woman who makes moves, who makes love to him, who's aggressive when he wants her to be; but in truth, most men want a woman to surrender to them fully and completely in the sexual act.

Some men describe women who do this as being capable of "complete abandonment," other men say that they hesitate admitting that they like to be the "dominant" one but that's what they do want, others will concede that they ultimately enjoy a "compliant" woman. This male reaction has nothing to do with any kind of abnormal S and M sex, it's simply the way gender differences have survived aeons and still exist today. The woman who acknowledges the concept of sexual surrender fills a man's ego need for conquest and power.

Women today are finally beginning to feel increasingly independent and equal in the workplace and in a wide range of other areas such as sports, politics, and the arts. Thus, it becomes singularly difficult to make a switch from liberated female to surrendering mate—even though it can and does entail exquisite physical and emotional pleasure for both partners. You're expected to be one person in the office and behind the wheel of a car, but in the bedroom many women make the mistake of disdaining the age-old role of the woman who gives and receives but ultimately surrenders herself to her mate.

The surrender switch is hard and may take some searching interior dialogue about your sense of feminine self in lovemaking; but if you aren't able to surrender—body and soul—to him, you can bet that the odds of non-monogamy are going to increase sharply. If you want a monogamous relationship, giving your man what he needs is what counts, and he needs to feel that he has you completely. The woman who's in bed with a man and holds back because of fear or anxiety about her own performance or, for example, her ability to have an orgasm or multiple orgasms, or the woman who begins to think about the children, the problems at the office, or her mother-in-law's latest unkind cut, cannot abandon herself to making love and cannot surrender herself to her mate because she's not really present sexually or emotionally. She's holding back from him by whirling around in her own anxieties and problems and those of others. Making a man feel you're totally involved, absolutely abandoned to the pleasures of the moment with him—you're wholly surrendering yourself to him—enhances his masculinity, thereby fulfilling one of those all-important basic ego needs.

Everything You Wanted to Know About Performance Anxiety

You've read over and over again that a man worries about having and keeping an erection. But do you really know what that means? Can a woman possibly imagine hav-

ing an uncontrollable, vulnerable—and measurable!
—organ outside her body moving of its own volition?
Sometimes it shoots up when you don't want it to, and
sometimes the damn thing won't budge, no matter how
much you pray that it will.

A woman simply cannot know how it feels to have to
perform, to visibly have an erection—it's close to in-
conceivable for us. Yet, if you ever hear a man honestly
express the fear and shame and helplessness it can cost
him, you can't help but see him in another light—a much
more compassionate one.

His penis is independent of him, he has no say whatsoever in its behavior. He's at the mercy of this external, exposed piece of flesh. And this experience has to
shape the fears he has and the ways he tries to hide
them—and the ways he deals with women.

Perhaps the most unwitting sexual mistake a woman
can make is to underestimate the terror—that is the appropriate word—every man feels at times about the many
uncertainties of his ungovernable organ. His penis, as
we've heard again and again through these pages, is tied
to his masculine ego. What women can so easily forget
is that the two are braided together in the same way that
sex and love are intertwined for us.

When men seem sexually inexplicable, or when they
retreat, or when they appear insensitive or callous, what
they could well be suffering from is the physical and emotional gridlock that comes from performance anxiety.
Under such a condition, very few men can tell you what's
bothering them because they feel they are exposing their
ultimate inadequacy. There's no such comparable physical experience for women. (A frigid woman may not
feel any physical pleasure, but it is not necessary for her
to perform.)

One of the men I interviewed explained, "A man who
says he has a headache or is overworked or who claims

he just wants to watch TV may be afraid that he won't be able to get it up. He's too anxious to tell his wife or girlfriend, but even more basic is that he certainly doesn't want to admit the possibility of failure to himself."

Note the word "failure," not being able to have an erection is equated with falling short of, being defeated, being deficient, inadequate. Consider having to face this set of emotions every time you set out to do something that should be enjoyable. Women too can feel failure in not achieving orgasm but some do save face by faking. A man has no such refuge.

Performance anxiety can lead disastrously quickly to temporary erection problems, and from there it can careen to chronic impotence. I've tried to emphasize the fears *every* man has at one time or another with performance anxiety because, in acknowledging this, women can more readily understand the delicacy of sexual activity for men. We tend to think of males as rough, randy, and perpetually ready. This is largely a fantasy—for both sexes—and one that we should put to rest. A woman who is aware of and empathizes with a man's sexual functioning is always going to be the better lover.

Confusing Love and Sex

Men constantly say that women confuse love and sex—and this causes big problems for both genders. It goes back to the equation in Chapter Two in which we saw that for the majority of men: Sex equals sex plus sometimes love. And for the majority of women: Sex equals love.

Another way of saying this is that many men describe themselves as enjoying sex as a purely physical experience, and at other times they are intensely emotionally as well as physically involved. Very few women will characterize a sexual experience without alluding to warmth, affection, romance, or some emotional connection.

"I think most men can experience two kinds of sex—with attachment and without," said an articulate twenty-seven-year-old. "Women that I know seem to have only one kind of sex—there is inevitably some kind of expectation or attachment to their partners."

"If a woman doesn't really comprehend that men can fuck their brains out without a moment's thought 'to the relationship' that's going to come out of it, then she really is making a mistake and shortchanging herself," he adds.

In sum, men are claiming that women make the "mistake" of not enjoying sex for its own sake but always conceive of it in love terms. This is not a mistake women are making, it's simply the logical fallout of the differences in male and female ego needs.

But is there any way to reconcile the age-old love/sex schism between men and women? The answer lies in both sexes understanding each other's psychosexual needs—and satisfying them. "A woman can indulge a man with simple, sweaty, hot workout sex," says one sex therapist, "as long as her mate replenishes her ego needs with romantic, warm, affectionate lovemaking. Everyone can get what they want out of sex—if they're willing to give."

The Sixth Deadly Sexual Mistake

If you ask a person "Is sex most important at the beginning of a relationship?" he or she will most likely answer "Sure." Take a random sampling of men and women, and you'll find that the majority would agree that the significance of sex decreases after the initial hullabaloo of passion dies down. Herein lie the seeds of a sure monogamy killer.

In 1976 a little-known study by R. Cimbalo, V. Faling, and P. Mousaw involved thirty-two couples. The results of this investigation were detailed in "The Course of Love: a Cross-Sectional Design" (*Psychological Reports*, 38, 1976). The researchers showed that *over time the importance of sex increased* and the value of security decreased.

In 1988 the highly respected psychologist Robert Sternberg confirmed these findings. "As habituation sets into a passionate relationship," he writes of a study he completed with Sandra Wright, "the couple's ability to sustain some spark of passion and an interesting sex life becomes more and not less important."

Of all the sexual "mistakes" you can make, not being constantly aware of this fact is the most dangerous. Knowing that sex is a bigger issue—it's a greater need—as time goes on, gives you an edge in maintaining a monogamous relationship because you're going to pay a lot more attention to having a satisfying sex life—for both of you.

One last cautionary word: If you think sex will devolve into boredom, the chances are that it absolutely will. Most adults seem to feel that sexual ennui is as much a marker of marriage as an anniversary. It's inevitable, so this thinking goes, passion cools, lovemaking—if it continues at all—becomes poky and predictable. What you *think will happen* in a marriage or relationship is a good indicator of what will *actually take place*. And these are not just idle words. Studies show that the most accurate predictors of how a marriage will turn out are the couple themselves. Ergo, if you forecast cloudy sexual skies, it's more than likely that sexual dissatisfaction will pour all over you. Sexual fallout is a self-generating prophecy. Adventurous, monogamous sex is not just somewhere over a rainbow, it's possible to experience throughout a lifetime.

SEVENTEEN

"I'll Never Forgive You!"

Like almost every other marriage, Suzanne and Dan Gunne's had its ups and downs, but Suzanne felt contented with her life—until she had a disastrous experience.

"Dan told me he had to go on a business trip to Detroit where some of his major accounts are," recalled Suzanne, a thirty-four-year-old mother of two. "Both kids were away on sleepovers and it was my best friend Jan's birthday. We decided to celebrate by going to the finest restaurant in town."

"We were in top spirits when we arrived," Suzanne continued. "As we were walking to our table I noticed a man sitting at one of the corner booths. His head was tilted in a particular way, and he had his hand protectively over the hand of the woman he was with. Something in that romantic gesture reminded me of Dan, but *he* was in Detroit. As we were being seated I looked at the man again, and it was Dan. I couldn't believe it. Of course Jan saw him too—and the woman he was with. I can't describe the feelings I had. I was betrayed and sick with rage. I'll never forgive him."

Suppose the unforgivable becomes a reality. Your lover, your husband, has been unfaithful. The issue of monogamy is not a gnawing abstraction. Something terrible has actually happened to you. What do you do? Would you head straight for a divorce lawyer? Would you suffer in silence? Would you stay in the marriage but make life hell for him? Many women I interviewed had intolerable experiences like Suzanne's—and they felt they could never forgive their mates. What is the best way to cope with such a crisis? Is infidelity truly unforgivable?

To address this intelligently, it's important first to define specifically what is unforgivable. Clarifying terms is necessary because "the unforgivable" is tricky, and may mean different things to different people. But matrimonial lawyers and marriage counselors who deal with these kinds of problems on a daily basis are in fairly close agreement on what constitutes a truly unforgivable act.

What Is "Unforgivable"?

"Even though I've seen people learn to live with exceedingly upsetting situations, there are two offenses that I have found most patients cannot forgive," says Milton Pereira, M.D., a well-known New York psychiatrist, and a great many other professionals agree with his view.

The first "unforgivable" is sustained drug or alcohol abuse. A partner's addiction usually leads to an act of physical, verbal, or emotional abuse that is intolerable.

The second major unendurable act is the husband having not merely an affair, but a homosexual affair.

Kenneth Kemper, a matrimonial lawyer in New York, says, "A husband's admission of bisexuality is the most psychologically devastating experience a woman can have."

Such a revelation is a murderous blow to a woman's ego, not only because of the psychological menace but the physical one as well. Still, a married man having a gay relationship is quite rare, while heterosexual infidelity, despite the fears of AIDS and other sexually transmitted diseases, can be, as we've seen, oppressively commonplace.

Yet casual infidelity does not lead to the divorce lawyer's door as automatically as it did in the recent past. Most therapists and marriage counselors agree that the sexual permissiveness that has evolved in the last fifteen years has made such a sexual transgression relatively more acceptable: It has become an issue to deal with rather than the issue over which a relationship breaks up.

In Dr. Anthony Pietropinto's experience, adultery "doesn't come anywhere near being unforgivable." About 14 percent of the women in a survey Pietropinto conducted on the subject said they would choose "immediate divorce" as a consequence of infidelity. "Even then," he says, "we don't know if they would because that was a hypothetical question. It certainly holds, however, that long-term affairs are more unforgivable, more difficult to deal with, than a short-term fling or one-night stand."

Reactions

When the "unforgivable" has happened, we take a knockout punch to the ego. All our gender identity is reeling under the attack. She must be prettier/sexier/smarter than I am. What does he see in her? What's wrong with me? Why can't I be better for him? What did I do to make him have this affair? No man will ever love me again—these are the most common reactions to adultery.

He doesn't want me translates into one of the most powerful, painful forms of ego fracturing that we can suffer. On the heels of this feeling of acute rejection, loss of self-esteem, devaluation of self-worth, and even self-loathing can quickly follow.

"It's not your fault that he had an affair is what I tell patients who come to me during this kind of crisis," explains a New York psychotherapist. "It doesn't mean you're less of a woman, less of a person. You have the same set of good attributes as you had yesterday before you found out about the affair. You have not changed or become less worthy as a woman, as a human being. What has happened is something to be examined carefully—preferably with the aid of a competent professional—so that you can learn from the experience and, hopefully, benefit by it for your own ends."

Suzanne Gunne felt "a massive tidal wave of rejection" and then white-hot rage. "I screamed at him until he began to cry, and this is a man who has never before shed a tear, not even when his mother died."

While Suzanne's response was fury, which she vented directly at her husband, another woman might coldly withdraw as a way to punish her mate's intolerable act.

"We stayed together after I found out about his affair," a woman from Indianapolis told me, "but to this day we've never had sex again. It's been three years."

"Has he tried to have sex with you? Do you see this continuing—for the rest of your life?" I asked.

"He made some overtures about six months after I found out, but of course I didn't respond. What choice do I have?" she replied with no emotion in her voice. "I believe that I'll leave him when our last child is off at college, but that is nine years from now."

"How would you characterize your marriage at this point?" I wanted to know.

"We're civil. We cohabit. We're involved with the children. Except for that, the relationship is dead," she replied.

This woman's reaction is complete emotional withdrawal and a kind of martyrdom. By not trying in any way to resolve the problem, she clings to her rage and scorn to further distance herself from her husband and ends up hurting herself even more.

Such a long-suffering stance prevents this woman from seeking out the reasons that her husband has been unfaithful. Suzanne Gunne, on the other hand, felt she did want to make an effort to save her marriage.

"After it happened we had long talks, but we always ended up livid and even further apart," recalled Suzanne when we talked about the affair four months after it happened. "I felt there was no choice but to seek marriage counseling. We both finally decided to go and found it extremely helpful. I realized that even with all of Dan's outward confidence, he was afraid of many things. Specifically, he was tremendously worried that younger men would overtake him in his career and that he believed his professional life was collapsing. I began to see that his ego was very fragile—and you need to be tough in the kind of aggressive sales job he was in. I realized I wasn't at fault; he hadn't rejected me because I was not enough of a woman to keep him faithful. The thing with the other woman gave him some ego strength he needed—and when it happened, I didn't know the dynamics of the hungry ego, as you call it.

"Dan had only been seeing her for a month or so. Thank God I found out about it before he was too deeply entrenched. . . . We're working together on giving him inner fortification he needs from within the relationship so he doesn't have to go outside it."

Suzanne's hard-won understanding of Dan's ego needs

and her own helped to return the relationship to a
healthier equilibrium. Dan, too, shouldered some of the
responsibility, but Suzanne readily admits she was the
one who kept the marriage intact. "He would have let
me divorce him, I think," she said. "He was too weary
to make an effort to hold it all together, and of course
the other woman was there waiting for him to leave
me. I have two kids and a good life. I took a long time
to decide whether I loved him enough to go through
all that therapy and all that work. In the end, I decided
I did love him—and it *is* worth it."

Usually the first thing a therapist will do when a
woman like Suzanne seeks help is to bring her to understand what has happened in the relationship and why.

"First, look at the situation," says a Manhattan psychiatrist who deals with couples, "and ask yourself if
what he has done truly is unforgivable. What, specifically
are you reacting to? What needs of *yours* are not being
met? What needs of *his* aren't being fulfilled? Is there any
way his needs could be met? Or is he asking for the
impossible? Are you? Is it the act itself that is so heinous
or is it that something has been hidden from you? This
kind of thinking can help you clarify what is *realistically*
unacceptable."

If you can see that not every transgression is a total
calamity, a rejection of you as a woman, or signals the
end of a relationship, then you'll be in a better position
to assess your options. Matrimonial lawyers as well as
therapists point out that a long-term marriage can usually withstand more acute stress than a recent one. A
single act of infidelity is in itself usually not responsible
for divorce or breakup: a series of problems capped with
one last straw is what drives people to divorce attorneys.

What Are Your Options?

If he has been unfaithful, you have three roads open to you:

• You can decide to walk away from the relationship.

• You may choose to accept the situation.

• You can face the problem and try and work it out.

Jennifer Lang, a twenty-nine-year-old stockbroker, married for three years, opted for divorce. "I found out about Gene's year-long affair with his secretary," she said, "and even though he swore he'd fire her and never see her again, he didn't live up to his promise. I knew finally that he would continue to see her or someone else. He can't stay faithful, and that is something I just can't tolerate. I have a good job, and I'm going to find someone else and have the kind of relationship I want. He should get to a good shrink." Jennifer had realized that no matter what she did within the relationship, Gene's ego needs were impossible to satisfy, and her own need for monogamy and genuine intimacy could be fulfilled by another man.

To accept the situation—to stay in a relationship knowing that you cannot wipe the slate clean—is another option—and perhaps the most difficult to choose. Again, it is a painful matter of weighing certain factors, discovering what you can live with, and recognizing your decision as being the best one for you at the time.

"At first, when I found out what was going on, I felt I couldn't live with him and I couldn't live without him," recalls a woman whose live-in lover of three years had a "short-term affair" with a fellow lawyer. "That feeling of ambivalence was the worst torture of all. It took me months to tip the scale to the point where I admitted I couldn't live without him and that we'd try and work it out. It may sound silly, but I made lists on yellow pads of what was good and bad about him, about me, about the relationship, and when I added it up, it was clear that it would be better for me to stay in the relationship. Of course, even after I had the lists, I still felt fury and betrayal at what had happened. But once I made up my mind I wanted it to work, I felt better about it and we're working it out. What I really want is to marry Jim, and I think that this whole affair has blown our relationship wide open and, because of all our talking, we've gotten much closer and marriage is much more of a possibility."

It can also be helpful to know that you don't have to forgive, said one specialist in marriage-related crises. Many of us were reared on the forgive-and-forget ethic, she points out, and this kind of thinking can add extra psychological stress. "Maybe you can't forgive," she says, "but you can go on."

Confrontation, which many women feel is essential for sanity and as a release for pent-up feelings, may not be necessarily beneficial either. There are times when it's better not to talk about what happened. Instead of re-couping emotional ground, a confrontation may simply result in losing more of one's already shaky self-esteem and taking another ego battering. Rather than risking a shattering face-to-face challenge, it can be far wiser to add up the attractions of the relationship, decide if it's worth it to throw out what you have invested and what your realistic options for the future are.

"It's a very rough world out there," says another psychotherapist. "A person may simply not have the courage to do what they feel is traditionally the 'right' thing—that is, split up or divorce—in the face of infidelity. Perhaps after measured consideration, she will make the choice to stick with the marriage because she's getting other very important benefits out of it.''

The third option, when faced with a situation that seems insoluble and irreconcilable, is tackling the problem with your partner. Again, certain guidelines can be helpful.

Begin by accepting the possibility that the act of infidelity is not necessarily unforgivable. Then set aside some time to talk together. You don't have to feel you're condoning his action simply because you're talking about it. Almost nothing he can say at this time can justify what he's done, but talking, in most cases, will help. Begin with a short discussion that is confined simply to going over the facts of the situation. Then, at another time, move on from the facts to areas you have questions about. Some therapists recommend setting a specific limit to these discussions. Ten to fifteen minutes is often a time prescription.

''This kind of talking,'' points out Dr. Milton Pereira, a respected New York psychiatrist, ''has to be done without making it a war. You want to solve a problem, not create more tension.''

As you continue to talk together, stick to the facts and your questions about them in the most neutral, positive way that you can. While this process is taking place, Dr. Pereira suggests ''dipping into safe areas in the past that you can try to re-experience. Go out for walks, for drives. Go back to your favorite restaurant, see intimate friends. Don't venture into the deep waters of a relationship discussion without taking a life preserver of the good times and the warm feelings with you.''

If you're so enraged that you can't see straight, WAIT, Dr. Pereira cautions, *don't talk about it*. Ask yourself what in the past have you done to help blow off steam—and then do it. Then, when you're in as neutral a frame of mind as possible, begin talking about the facts only and move on, very slowly, to the more painful questions you need to ask in order to clarify what happened and to begin to defuse the anger and resentment.

Some therapists feel it is better to deliver a monologue than to engage in a perilous dialogue no matter how short. After each person has had their say, a couple can then begin to talk together. First, however, they should talk separately.

Maggie Scarf details this kind of therapeutic approach in *Intimate Partners*. Each member of the couple agrees to a "task": one person talks for a period of time (half an hour) without interruption from the other. (Who goes first can be a matter of a toss of a coin or alphabetical order of names.) The other person's task is to listen with undivided attention. At the end of the time period there is no discussion, no judgment on what has been said. Next, the other member of the couple does the talking for the same period of time, and the partner listens. This kind of structured exercise, underscores Scarf, "can provide an entry into a new way of being together." Although deceptively simple, the task is a "remarkably effective" way to initiate change when a relationship is stuck, especially in the quicksand of infidelity.

The Ultimatum Trap

Don't box yourself into a corner with an ultimatum, advise the majority of therapists. It's unwise to say "If you see that woman one more time, I'll leave you," unless you really mean it. It may not be possible for him to break it off unless he sees her one more time, so be chary of challenging with an ultimatum—you may find yourself losing face or, far worse, stuck with a condition or requirement that you're ultimately sorry for. Letting him know clearly that this is an act you don't want repeated, one that you cannot tolerate—without issuing an ultimatum—is usually the safer course of action.

"Don't expect him to immediately end everything. What usually happens is that he feels 'torn,' " explains a pastoral counselor who has helped many couples through infidelity. "Some women feel it's the lying that's the most hurtful," she explains. "But he had to lie. You can't expect him to tell the truth in this situation. Many women concentrate on the lying instead of the infidelity, which *is* bad. It doesn't mean he is totally untrustworthy, he had to lie to cover something he did. You've got to look at the whole picture, not just the lying."

Another unpleasant truth is that the "other woman" is a problem both members of the couple have to deal with. She's *there*, she's reality, you both have to acknowledge her. You can't simply say, "she's your problem" and let it go at that. True, it's his responsibility to deal with the other woman, say the professionals, but don't deny she exists; it will cause further pain and halt the healing process.

Working on any problem together takes time, commitment, and determination, and this is doubly true when the problem is infidelity. But if both of you are willing to face the realities of acutely painful emotions, the rate of success, according to the experts, is high. When faced with the unforgivable, a couple may be surprised to find they can learn a great deal about themselves that is of real substance and value in maintaining the relationship.

EIGHTEEN

Diamonds and Orange Juice

Researching and writing on monogamy has been challenging, stimulating, provocative—and rewarding. As a result of the past two years of work I think I have a better understanding of what makes men and woman tick—I've learned a great deal that I can use in my own life, and I hope I've passed on some of these insights to you. Most of my interviews, as I said, came about through the suggestions of friends, colleagues, and acquaintances. Several happened from chance meetings and coincidences. The two in this last chapter took place in unexpected and unusual circumstances, and I think they sum up many of the ideas that I've tried to get across in the previous pages.

I have a fondness for jewelry—especially the kind I can't afford. There's a very special shop in California that has the most beautiful stuff: lovely spills of antique pearls with delicate clasps, stately rings of rare emeralds and sapphires, an Indian princess's rose brooch fashioned from rubies with golden leaves that actually tremble—all these delights and many more are to be found under the heavy glass in the burnished burled cases of this fabulous emporium.

I was working in Los Angeles and happened upon Mr. Wolfe and his treasures while I was on my way to conduct an interview at the Beverly Wilshire Hotel. I had stopped to gaze at the objects in Mr. Wolfe's window. As I stood there, a man stepped out of the shop. You couldn't help but notice him, as he had on a gray pin-striped suit that contrasted sharply with the pale blue and white workout gear and leisure outfits that were in evidence along Rodeo Drive at two in the afternoon. He was tucking a small—very small—moroccan leather box into his jacket pocket. He looked like a movie star.

I continued scanning the lovely pieces in the window when a charm caught my eye. It was a heart of pearls and would be a perfect birthday present for my mother. I entered the store to ask the price and fell under the spell of Mr. Wolfe's wares. Not only did I ask to see the heart, I shamelessly asked him to drag out bracelets and necklaces that I knew I would never buy. But he was charming and delighted to show me anything I desired. We got to chatting. I told him I was from New York and adored his store and the unusual things he'd collected.

"Did you see the fellow that just left?" he inquired.

I nodded yes.

"Well, he's from New York, too, and some woman is going to be very happy at what he just walked out with."

"And what was that?" I asked.

"I had purchased a very unusual diamond," Mr. Wolfe said. "It was of a cut I've only seen once or twice in thirty years. A shallow, very flat diamond, smaller than a baby's nail, and it was set in a ring with baguettes all the way round it. It was absolutely dazzling in an understated way, a unique piece. Mr. Leahy saw it in the window, came in, and asked if it could be engraved in two days. That was difficult enough to pull off in such an amount of time but then he told me what he wanted engraved and I didn't think it was possible."

He stopped, waiting for me to ask for the punchline.

"So what did he want engraved?" I obliged him.

"LOVEX∞" and he wrote the characters on a pad of paper.

"Code?" I asked conspiratorially.

"He never explained what it meant," Mr. Wolfe said, "but damn if he didn't want the words engraved *on the face of the diamond!*"

"That's not possible, is it?" I asked, adding, "though it's an interesting idea."

"I told him I'd seen coats of arms incised on rubies and emeralds and sapphires—all soft stones—but never on a diamond.

"He asked me to find a craftsman who could do it—in two days if you can believe it—because he was leaving LA then and this was a very important present. Well, to make a long story short, I happen to have the perfect engraver here in Culver City, and he took it as the challenge of his life to do that to the diamond. He had to perform the work under a microscope. Like a neurosurgeon. And so Mr. Leahy, who you just saw walking out of my store, has one of the most beautiful, most unusual rings in the world. Or, rather I should say, Mr. Leahy's friend will have it."

What kind of a man thinks of *engraving a diamond?* I wondered as I hurried down Rodeo so I'd be on time for my appointment.

Two days later I was in LAX waiting for American's noon flight to Kennedy, and I saw him—the man with the ring from Mr. Wolfe's—wearing the same gray pin-striped suit. He was reading *The Bonfire of the Vanities.*

I sat next to him and pulled out my notepad to read over some of the material from the Los Angeles interviews. We had about a half hour's wait for the plane and I decided to check in with my office. As I was on hold for someone in New York, he came over to the wall of phones and placed a credit card call. Then he Touch-Toned another number, this time hunching his broad shoulders into the metal fins that separated his telephone from mine. I could tell from the softness of his voice that it was a very intimate conversation.

We returned to our seats and he smiled in a friendly way. I began to pull out my notepad again when an announcement was made that our flight would be delayed by at least an hour.

"Everything is late these days," he said amiably, checking his watch.

"Have you read this?" he asked, pointing to the title on the cover of his book.

We fell to talking. His name was Richard Leahy and he was a partner in a small graphic design firm in New York and had been supervising an important corporate logo job in Los Angeles. I told him I was working on monogamy.

"Now *that's* an interesting subject," he said, unabashed. "Tell me more."

"No, you tell me," I said, "are you monogamous?"

"Absolutely monogamous," he replied.

"What do you mean by that?"

"What else would I mean but that I've been married for ten years and never screwed around once. Isn't that what is normally meant by monogamy?"

"Yes," I said, smiling, "but some men don't see it that way."

"Well, I don't go around shouting that I'm monogamous from the top of the Empire State Building. Tell me, I'm curious. How many monogamous men did you find in your research?"

"Well, about a third were monogamous," I said, "but it seemed as if there were many more unfaithful men. I think it's because they're more verbal about the subject, they almost want to brag about it. And have *you* suffered the pain of temptation?"

"Of course I've been tempted," he replied, returning my grin. "I don't consider it a hardship but a privilege to be monogamous."

"You sound poetic."

"I don't talk about it much, as I said," he responded, turning thoughtful, "but I had an unusual experience this week in LA, and it made me think about monogamy as I never had before.

"I know that women are attracted to me, I don't want to sound immodest, but it happens to be so. I think it's because I genuinely like their company and they get the message by some sort of osmosis. My partner and I have been having complicated times in the financial area—are you sure you really want to hear this?"

"I very much want to," I answered, "but would it deter you if I made some notes?"

"For your book?"

"Yes, if you don't mind. I have a feeling you're going to say something interesting." The diamond ring nestled in his pocket or in his beat-up attaché case was already intriguing enough—I definitely wanted to know more.

"It's amazing how easy it is to talk to strangers, isn't it?"

"It's a well-documented phenomenon," I said seriously, " 'the strangers on a train syndrome.' A research psychologist out in Minnesota did some work on it, I think."

"Strangers on a plane," he said, smiling. He was borderline flirtatious.

"You were saying that you were having a hard time at work and that this had something to do with monogamy—"

"Oh yes, well, since the stock market crash, business has been very dicey. And I admit I've been nervous about it. Julie, my wife, has been under terrible strain too. She's a molecular biologist working day and night on the AIDS virus. I see her for five minutes in the morning if I'm lucky. This has been going on for three months."

"And you haven't had sex."

"How did you know that?"

"I hear it all the time—and I'm not being facetious."

"Julie always wants to make love, even if it's just a slam-bam; she really likes sex. It was me that had the problem. For five months—or more—I didn't feel like a sexual being. Being thirty-nine—mid-life crisis time—and having real financial setbacks was something new to a superachiever like me." He grinned ruefully and studied a wide-bodied 707 through the window as it backed out of its gate directly in front of us.

"Anyway," he continued, "I've always had a strong sex drive. And I was worried. Was I losing it?"

"By any chance had you been impotent with your wife?"

"Are you a mindreader? Yeah, something like that happened a couple of times before she started on her marathon work schedule. How did you know?"

"Because every man has trouble at one time or another. And it's very frightening. And I've talked to plenty of sex therapists about the problem. You don't have an erection one time and you think, oh God, I'm going to have trouble again. And you do—because you're so worried about it. A vicious cycle begins. You think you won't have an erection. So you back off from sex. You tell yourself you're just not interested or your wife's too busy, but the real reason is that you're afraid you won't be able to perform. And your wife is bewildered and doesn't know what's happening because you're too afraid to tell her—or yourself—but tell me more about what happened to you in Los Angeles."

He had been watching me intently while I explained all this and then looked away. "Well anyway," he said, after a long moment's reflection, "I was staying at the Four Seasons hotel in order to give the client the impression that the firm was doing very well—I can't believe I'm telling you all these personal things."

"It's okay. You'll be disguised in the book, if I use this. Don't worry. You really can trust me."

"Have you been to the Four Seasons? Do you know the bar there?"

"No, but I can imagine it," I said.

"I was waiting for the client and this woman slips right onto the chair next to me. And she says, 'How do you feel about ordering champagne for us?' And then she laughs. This incredible, feminine, charming laugh. Now women have been flirtatious, but this has never happened to me before and you have to believe me that she was about the most beautiful woman I've ever laid eyes on. Julie, my wife, is an authentic knockout, but this woman even ranked above her. Turns out she is doing this on a dare from her friend. They've been sitting two tables away watching me wait for the client and Janey—that was her name—is really a bundle of mischief. Not only is she devastatingly beautiful, she has a brain. She's a network correspondent in LA and had worked in the governor's office before that."

"So did you order the champagne?"

"I told her I was on the verge of an important meeting and if she and her friend were around later, I could have a drink."

"Did you think of sleeping with her?"

"I didn't have time to think because the client had arrived. But I did know that I had a hard-on. The first one I'd had in months. And she was the cause of it."

"But even though you're monogamous, hadn't that ever happened before in relation to another woman? And you quelled the urge?"

"It had never happened before. I never thought about cheating, there was no need to. I love Julie. It's very difficult to say this," he said, concentrating on the slow-moving tail of an incoming aircraft, "but I wanted to know that it would happen again. It wasn't happening with Julie and I didn't know why."

"So you'd risk being unfaithful to see if you were physically able to have sex," I said, empathizing with his problem.

"It was that crucial to me, yes," he admitted. "The only way I can explain this is that I needed to know I was a man. It was vitally important."

"And then what?"

"The client liked the work, we landed the contract. And I went to my room to call her so we could meet in the bar. I had two things to celebrate—a hard-on and a new job. But when I picked up the phone, I stopped and took out the picture of Julie that I carry in my wallet and I looked at it for a long time."

He broke off and I said nothing, hoping that he would go on without my asking.

"I consider myself a thoughtful man," he said. "I've always had a quest, something to achieve, mountains to climb. When I thought about it, I realized the reason I was having problems with sex was that I was letting work and achieving goals get in the way and I was not paying enough attention to Julie and the relationship. I suddenly saw that everything would be okay sexually when I got home. I could explain all this to Julie. She's always been with me every centimeter of the way, no matter how tough her own work is. She's supportive and loving and caring in ways I've never dreamed possible from another person. And I hope I've done the same for her too."

I smiled at his intensity and his disarming earnestness. He smiled in return and said, "I sat in my room and thought about Julie. All those years I never needed to be unfaithful, I had her there all the time; but there was still more about her to discover, I had her depths to plumb. I had the deep pleasure of knowing—really knowing—another person. I believe the greatest quest for two people is marriage. It's the greatest risk, the ultimate adventure."

"But what about your own personal Everests?" I asked.

"I'm just a guy," he said simply. "I don't want to stop being an explorer or race winner. I know that about myself. But I am also a human being. And the richest gift I can be given is the gift of sharing my life with another human being and, if I am lucky, with children."

Neither of us spoke. Down on the runway silvered planes, engines impatient to roar, gleamed in the early afternoon sun.

"So what happened with the other woman?" I said softly.

"I called Julie and she wasn't at home. So I phoned Janey, the woman from the bar, and asked her to meet me," he said.

I raised my eyebrows. A disappointment was coming.

"I ordered us champagne. And then I told her that I was married and that I was a monogamous man, and I loved my wife and that I couldn't cheat on her. And that she, as a woman, would want a husband like that. Now that I think about it, I must have sounded like a sentimental fool, but I wanted someone to know how important it was. I'm a very good judge of people and down

deep I knew she would respond in a positive way to
what I was saying."

"You do understand women," I said.

"No one does," he said, flashing a big grin that wid-
ened into the cat-ate-the-canary variety when he added,
"but I know a lot of them like jewelry."

"And I know you have a ring in your pocket," I said
absolutely straight-faced.

"You're not a journalist. You're a psychic."

I told him I'd seen him coming out of Mr. Wolfe's
and how the jeweler had described the extraordinary
etched stone. "But what did you inscribe on it and how
did you ever think of doing that to a diamond?"

"It came to me when I saw it in the window the night
after all that happened in the hotel. A diamond is very
beautiful and also very hard. So is marriage. I wanted
to tell Julie I knew that and I know what she's been
to me."

"What was the inscription?" I asked.

"The stone is not much larger than a caviar egg. I'm
a designer so I had to come up with a clever solution."
He took my pen and wrote LOVEX∞ on my notepad.

"Love followed by an x, which stands for multiply,"
he explained, "followed by an infinity sign. Love mul-
tiplied by infinity means 'I love you forever.' That's what
I'm saying to Julie. I couldn't etch it on Everest, so I
thought a diamond would do."

Not long after Richard Leahy told me that wonderful
story, I found myself telling a woman I'd just met at a
cocktail party about the etched diamond. She and I had
been introduced and I had commented on an unusual
antique brooch she was wearing, whereupon she confessed
that she was a jewelry maven and I recounted the meeting
with Richard at Mr. Wolfe's shop and at the airport. That
got us to talking about jewelry—and men.

"I just got a divorce nine weeks ago," she told me, "and it's tough going out there. Not too many nice guys around. The good ones—like the man you just told me about—are married, the others are usually gay."

"I hear that all the time," I nodded in agreement.

"As a matter of fact," she tensed up and turned to the doorway, "that's my ex-husband just coming in."

"Why don't we move into the other room," I suggested.

"No, no," she responded, looking directly at him and even more intensely at the woman accompanying him, a standout redhead in an expensive figure-revealing sweater and very short leather skirt.

The hostess gestured toward the bedroom so that the date could stow her jacket there, and the ex-husband walked straight toward us.

"Diana," he said uneasily, never taking his eyes off hers, "it's good to see you. I thought you might be here." I could feel the tension pulsating in the space between them.

"Please excuse me," I said, after she introduced us, "I'm going to get a refill for my drink. I'll talk to you later, Diana."

I left the party soon after, but I ran into Diana a week later at Tiffany's where we were both buying wedding presents for friends. We laughed at how appropriate it was that we ran into each other in a jewelry store and ended up by having a cappuccino together.

Our first conversation stands out in my mind because it so well illustrates how an intelligent, sophisticated woman's lack of awareness of men's ego needs and her own ego needs can lead to the disaster of divorce. A second conversation with Diana two months later yielded a move on her part that I think you'll find as surprising—and terrific—as I did.

"Greg—your ex-husband, what does he do?" I

asked when we'd settled into the booth at the coffee shop.

"He's in the import-export business, very successful for a thirty-six-year-old. He and I met at Stanford. I was an undergraduate and he was in the business school. We got married six months after we met," she replied.

"I would have thought he was an actor, he's so good-looking," I said.

"He's actually done a lot of TV commercials. He needed the money to get through school."

"Was he monogamous, do you think?" I asked.

"He always had women—and men—hitting on him especially when he was doing the TV stuff. Women would come on to him, men would come on to him—it made me nuts, but I realized it was something I had to live with. But he swore he never followed through, and I believed him."

"What do you think caused you two to split up?" I asked.

"Well, it actually was another woman," she admitted, "but he told me they never had sex together and I'm positive it's true."

"More explanation is needed here," I smiled and ordered another cinnamon roll.

"I found a sales slip in his suit pocket. It was for jewelry—wouldn't you know. But I'd never received any goody from Cartier. I confronted him and he admitted it was for this other woman. . . . One of the problems in this marriage was that he'd stopped being romantic. He used to give me presents all the time and all that seemed to end too. . . ."

"Go on," I said, after a few moments of silence between us.

"Well, sex had always been unbelievable for us. But even that stopped. He was too tired, too busy getting the business on its feet, too wiped out from traveling.

He had all sorts of excuses. We had sex about once a month, and I always felt he was doing me a favor and he was never really *there*. So when I saw this sales slip from Cartier, I went absolutely nuts, out of control. I knew it was another woman. And I went straight to a divorce lawyer."

"Didn't you two talk about what happened before you headed for the lawyer?" I asked.

"We had one long talk. But it didn't make much difference and it didn't make much sense to me. I was so angry, I probably couldn't hear him. He said something about orange juice, that he'd wished I'd brought him orange juice in the morning. Apparently, he had actually spent the night with this woman and had decided he couldn't have sex with her, he'd be betraying me, but she brought him orange juice in bed in the morning. And that's when he went out and got her a whatever it was from Cartier."

"Wait a minute," I said. "We're in the latter part of the 1980s—this doesn't add up. You didn't talk to him about what happened? The man hadn't even had sex with this woman and you got a divorce? Did you consider seeing a therapist?"

"He wouldn't talk. To me or a therapist. He wouldn't say anything except for this damn orange juice bit. He never talked much anyway. I'd had it. He wouldn't open up with me. I work hard too, you know. I didn't think I should have to make all the effort to keep this relationship going. I got tired of trying to make him talk and respond and tired of being the one who wanted sex and tired of—"

"Can I tell you something?" I interrupted. I then explained Dr. Train's theory about ego needs and the hungry ego. "It sounds," I said, "as if he needed some nurturing and this woman gave it to him symbolically by offering him orange juice."

I thought back to Chris, and to Gina Walker making him meat loaf and telling him he was the best lover and the best deal maker, and I told Diana what had happened to me.

"Here you have a guy," I went on, "who's typical in many ways. He doesn't talk much, he's tired from working so hard, his ego takes a daily beating in trying to make it to the top. Where he's not typical is that he's so attractive and he has easy access to women. But he loved you so much, he never took anyone up on their sexual offers and, as you said, he had *plenty* of opportunity. Seems to me that he could have had sex with the orange juice woman, but he loved you too much to do it."

"But he went and bought her an extravagant present. He didn't do that for me—and that's what I needed—not the present, the attention. He takes me for granted."

"Think of it this way," I said. "The gift he gave to that woman might have been a grateful thank-you for understanding what he needed instead of a sexual thank-you, which would have betrayed his wife. He was, in essence, sending you a message and that's really why he left the sales slip in his pocket for you to so easily find. I know it sounds like facile psychologizing, but I believe that a man's too clever to leave a paper trail of his infidelities unless he's trying to tell you something. And do you remember that man I told you about, the one with the etched diamond? He hadn't had sex with his wife for months—because he was afraid he'd be impotent. He was under so much pressure, he just couldn't perform, so he shied away from her. Maybe that was a problem with Greg too."

"I never thought of it from that angle," she admitted.

"May I be even more presumptuous—?"

"Sure, why not," she said with a grin.

"I have a hunch you're still in love with him."

"Being in love with him doesn't mean I can live with him. And we're divorced!"

"Was the divorce ugly?"

"No, amazingly not. We did a no-fault. He just moved out. We agreed that neither of us wanted any hassle and it was over. Just like that. He's called me three or four times and wanted to have dinner, but I said no. What's the use of going back to something that will end just the same way."

"So you haven't really raked each other over the coals with rancor, and it's possible that he still loves you, yes? And have you found anyone as attractive to you as he is?"

"Mmmm," she said noncommittally, then added, "But he's sure fucking a lot of women. You saw that date of his."

"Why shouldn't he? Sex is a way to make his ego feel good. You know," I added, "I've really come to believe that if a woman wants to make a relationship work, she's got to take the responsibility for it. It's not fair in the grand scheme of things, but that's the way it is. If a woman wants the kind of love you're talking about, she's going to have to be the one to make it work—or at least get things started. Why don't you give him a call and see what happens?"

Diana took this in and adroitly changed the subject. She was editing a series of travel books and wanted to know my favorite city, and did I have any restaurants to recommend?

I thought a good while about Diana after that talk. She and Greg are a classic example of today's male/female schism. She needs affection, romance, intimacy, and monogamy from him, and he needs some understanding from her both sexually and emotionally in order to give her the kind of love she wants. She's a contemporary liberated woman and doesn't want to "cater" to his whims of orange juice in bed if she isn't getting what she needs, which is his sexual attention and intimacy.

They were deadlocked. She felt he should do something about the relationship, since he was the one who was retreating from the intimacy and romance they'd had before. He, for his part, couldn't articulate his needs. He ended up sending a jumbled message by leaving the sales slip in his pocket and mumbling about orange juice in bed when Diana confronted him.

About four months later, I was talking to a friend on the phone and she said, "Did you hear that Diana Fallon got married?"

"No," I said, "she wasn't even seeing anyone the last time I talked with her. Who's the guy?"

"Her ex-husband, Greg Fallon."

I hung up the phone and immediately dialed Diana's office number.

"I'm personally and professionally interested," I began. "Why did you remarry your husband?"

She laughed and said, "Meet you for coffee late today?"

We sat over another cappuccino and she told me what had happened since I'd last talked with her.

"What you told me was not falling on deaf ears," she said. "I had thought a lot about that damn orange juice and what it symbolized. I never really knew why Greg and I got divorced. I just got so angry that I didn't take any time to think or to analyze. I finally called him and we had dinner.

"We ended up in bed. It was terrific. He spent the night. I made him fresh orange juice in the morning.

"I said to myself, what a small thing to do to make someone happy. Mornings are really hard for Greg. He has a tough time waking up and getting going. He needs all the help he can get. Doing the orange juice has tenderness and a feminine aspect to it, which I think was missing on my side because I resented not getting what

I wanted from him. I was expecting all the tenderness and romance to start with him. Orange juice is giving him some love and tenderness on a daily basis. And in return we've had better sex and a much more open relationship. I don't have to dance around in baby dolls to turn him on, and even if that's what he wanted, I'd consider it. I saw him in a whole different light, and, as a result, I think he began to respond to me in a much more loving way."

"So how did the marriage come about?" I asked.

"He never went back to his apartment after that night. As a matter of fact, I told him about our conversation and the man with the etched diamond. About a month later, he brought home a box with a ring in it." She paused and smiled.

"It wasn't etched but was just a plain gold band with a card that said 'Will you marry me?' tucked into the top of the box. And we got married again down at City Hall. We came home and celebrated with champagne and, of course, orange juice."

SMART WOMEN, FOOLISH CHOICES

by Dr Connell Cowan & Dr Melvyn Kinder

Why do so many bright, successful, interesting women end up with the wrong men?

In SMART WOMEN, FOOLISH CHOICES, clinical psychologists Dr Cowan and Dr Kinder offer much-needed insights and advice for the growing number of 'smart' women who have everything going for them but satisfying personal relationships.

Women can be drawn to the wrong men for a number of subtle yet powerful reasons. Unrealistic expectations, the conflict between independence and the need to be taken care of, and a lack of understanding of the male psyche are just some of the causes of frustration and disappointment in love.

SMART WOMEN, FOOLISH CHOICES shows women how to open new opportunities and make their relationships happier, how to recognise the men they need, and how to understand what *really* causes men to fall in love. It gives every woman the chance to discover a new way of looking at men, relationships, and the possibilities of lasting fulfillment with the opposite sex.

'A wondrously sensitive, no-nonsense guide'
WEST COAST REVIEW OF BOOKS

'A fascinating and helpful book'
LOS ANGELES TIMES

0 553 17202 6

MEN WHO HATE WOMEN AND THE WOMEN WHO LOVE THEM

by Dr S. Forward & J. Torres

IS THIS THE WAY LOVE IS SUPPOSED TO FEEL?

- Does the man you love assume the right to control how you live and behave?

- Have you given up important activities or people to keep him happy?

- Is he extremely jealous or possessive?

- Does he switch from charm to anger without warning?

- Does he belittle your opinions, your feelings or your accomplishments?

- Does he withdraw love, money, approval, or sex to punish you?

- Does he blame you for everything that goes wrong in the relationship?

- Do you feel yourself 'walking on eggs' and apologizing all the time?

If the questions here reveal a familiar pattern, you may be in love with a misogynist – a man who loves you, yet causes you tremendous pain because he acts as if he hates you.

In this superb self-help guide, Dr Susan Forward draws on case histories and the voices of men and women trapped in these relationships to help you understand your man's destructive pattern, the part you play in it, how to break the pattern, heal the hurt, regain your self-respect, and either rebuild your relationship or find the courage to love a truly loving man.

0 553 17451 7

WOMEN MEN LOVE, WOMEN MEN LEAVE

by Dr Connell Cowan & Dr Melvyn Kinder

UNDERSTANDING PASSION AND COMMITMENT

From the bestselling authors whose SMART WOMEN/FOOLISH CHOICES became the indispensable guide for millions of single women comes the long-awaited answer to every woman's most pressing question: What do men *really* want? What makes a man fall in love with a woman and want to stay with her forever?

In this follow-up, clinical psychologists Dr Connell Cowan and Dr Melvyn Kinder help women understand men better: what attracts men; what turns men off: and what male/female 'chemistry' is all about. They demonstrate through numerous case studies those attitudes and behaviour patterns that elicit negative responses in men. For example, men may fear women who are overly dependent on them, or women who use aggressive seduction techniques. They also offer insights into the behaviours that evoke loving and positive responses in men.

Contrary to what many women think, men are eager to commit; they are usually attracted to strong women with whom they can have a challenging relationship, and they have an often unspoken but compelling need for friendship.

WOMEN MEN LOVE/WOMEN MEN LEAVE is a book for all women seeking to understand what 'chemistry' is all about – and how to create it and keep it alive!

0 553 17590 4

A SELECTION OF NON-FICTION TITLES
AVAILABLE FROM CORGI AND BANTAM BOOKS